川越の伝説

発行：川越を英語で歩こう会
発売：仙波書房

表紙・イラスト　宮内茂

First published in Kawagoe by the Kawagoe English Walkers
2-15-1 Semba-machi, Kawagoe-shi, Saitama 350-0034

Copyright © 2024 The Kawagoe English Walkers
All rights reserved. No part of this publication may be reproduced, stored in a retrieval system, or transmitted, in any form or by any means, without the prior written permission of the copyright holder.

Translated and published by the Kawagoe English Walkers.
Edited and supervised by Miyauchi Shigeru,
Leader of the Kawagoe English Walkers.
Illustrated by Miyauchi Shigeru.

Special thanks to
Mr. Ikehara Shoji, the writer of the original stories in Japanese
and the Board of Education in Kawagoe.

FORWARD

This book is the fruit of the kind and wonderful cooperation of many people who were concerned in this project enthusiastically.

First I would like to express my sincerest thanks to Mr. Ikehara Shoji, the writer of the original stories of "Kawagoe Legends-川越の伝説" and "Sequel to Kawagoe Legends-続 川越の伝説," and to the Board of Education of Kawagoe City for letting us use the original manuscript as the text.

Legends are sometimes very fuzzy and contain some incoherence. But legends are not always a pack of lies. There is certainly some truth or fact we should not forget or ignore. Legends vaguely imply to us what we should do or what we should not do by showing historical facts, warnings, examples and teachings. That is why legends have been handed down from generation to generation.

Let me tell you one surprising story that proves legends have some unbelievable power. Some years ago I used the copy of "Kawagoe Legends" as a textbook at a school for nurses. One woman student in her thirties said to me, "At first I didn't understand why we should read legends and I didn't want to read them because they have nothing to do with our work. But I recently had one amazing experience at the day-care center where I work. There is an old man who was not a people person, because he was stubborn, unsociable, defiant, never smiled, etc. But one day when I said something about a legend of his hometown, which I learned in the class, he unexpectedly smiled and began to talk about other legends he knew. In addition, he began to talk smilingly with anyone he sees after that. I'm quite sure that a legend has a power to change people completely. Now I understand why you made us read legends. Thanks a lot."

Fortunately, our city of Kawagoe has so many interesting legends. We chose 61 stories out of them and translated them into English hoping to add another dimension to Kawagoe's culture and to cover another aspect hidden behind the surface.

In translating the stories we exerted much effort to describe atmosphere of the originals as faithfully as possible.

Nothing will please me more if this book brings pleasure of reading legends to all the readers.

Miyauchi Shigeru
Leader, the Kawagoe English Walkers
October, 2024

CONTENTS

1.	Myojo-no Sugi and Myojo-no-Ike	明星の杉と明星の池	8
2.	The Main Temple called Cho'on Den	潮音殿	10
3.	No Bell Ringing at the Kitain Temple (No.1)	山内禁令（その一）	12
4.	No Bell Ringing at the Kitain Temple (No.2)	山内禁令（その二)	14
5.	No Bell Ringing at the Kitain Temple -An Angry Big Snake-	山内禁令（怒った大蛇）	15
6.	Three Foxes	三匹のキツネ	17
7.	The Tanuki in the Shape of a Boy	小僧に化けた狸	19
8.	The Hawks of Shoromon Gate	鐘楼門の鷹	21
9.	Pebbles on the Stone Lanterns	石灯ろうの小石	23
10.	Gohyaku Rakan, Five Hundred Statues of Rakan Saints	五百羅漢さま	25
11.	Dorobo-Bashi Bridge	どろぼう橋	26
12.	Enoki Inari	榎の木稲荷	28
13.	Bottomless Hole	底なしの穴	30
14.	The Unearthly Cedar Tree	お化け杉	32
15.	Biwa-Bashi Bridge	琵琶橋	34
16.	Kiri-fuki-no Ido	霧吹きの井戸	36
17.	The Sacrifice of a Maiden	人身御供	37
18.	Kataha-no-Ashi	片葉の葦	39
19.	Pebble-Throwing Service at the Yona-gawa River	よな川の小石供養	40
20.	Tenjin Mitarashi-no Seisui	天神洗足の井水	42

21.	Hatsukari-no Sugi	初雁の杉	44
22.	The Noise of Running Horses in the Castle	城中蹄の音	46
23.	The Gravestone of Mushi-kui Yakko	虫食い奴の墓	47
24.	The Story of the Bell at the Time Bell Tower	時の鐘のはなし	49
25.	The Bell at the Renkei-ji Temple	蓮馨寺の鐘	51
26.	Yukizuka Inari Fox Shrine	雪塚稲荷	53
27.	Kubo Inari Shrine	くぼ稲荷	54
28.	The Set of Three Images of Jizo Buddha	日ぎり三体地蔵さん	56
29.	Ocha Kanbo	お茶かんぼう	58
30.	The Tale of Go-no Kami	五の神のはなし	60
31.	Gigantic Snakes in Koike Pond	小池の大蛇	62
32.	Muddy-Footed Jizo-san	どろ足の地蔵さん	64
33.	Funa-zuka	船塚	66
34.	Fox at the Zenchu-ji Temple	善仲寺のキツネ	68
35.	Otoka-sama in Furuya Village	古谷のオトウカさま	70
36.	Horo Matsuri and Shishi-Gasira	ほろ祭りと獅子頭	71
37.	Kinome Choja	木野目長者	73
38.	Shishi-no-Miya and Mochi Rice Cake	獅子の宮さまとお餅	75
39.	Jihei-Zuka	次兵衛塚	77
40.	Inemuri-Zuka	いねむり塚	79
41.	Oiteke-Bori	おいてけ堀	81
42.	Exchanging Eggplants Ritual at Osuwa-sama Shrine	おすわさまのなすとりかえ	83
43.	Bunzo'emon, A Friend of Crying Children	泣く子もだまるぶんぞうえもん	85
44.	Hakusan-sama of Masukata	増形の白山さま	87

6

45	The Sixty-Six Burial Mounds in Matoba	的場六十六塚	89
46	Kompira-sama-no Tengu	こんぴらさまの天狗	91
47	Yonaki Jizo-san	夜泣き地蔵さん	93
48	A Tale of the Koaze-gawa Rive	小畔川のはなし	95
49	Hitotsume-Kozo of the River Koaze-gawa	小畔川の一つ目小僧	97
50	Kojiro of the Koaze-gawa River	小畔川の小次郎	99
51	A Story about the Toge-Bashi Bridge	とげ橋のいわれ	101
52	The Hackberry Tree with Warts	いぼ榎	103
53	Kappa's Visit to the Ise Jinja Shrine	かっぱの伊勢まいり	105
54	A Shugenja and a Fox	しゅげん者と狐	106
55	The Set of Bowls of the Bottomless Pond	底なし沼の膳椀	108
56	Ibo Jizo-san	いぼ地蔵さん	110
57	Goze-bashi Bridge	ゴゼ橋	112
58	Kita-muki Fudo-sam	北向き不動さま	113
59	Mr. Tengu of the Kosai-ji Temple	広済寺の天狗様	115
60	Shabuki-Babah	しゃぶきばばあ	116
61	EXTRA -2 versions of Minbu Inari -A-	民部稲荷	118
62	EXTRA -2 versions of Minbu Inari -B-	民部稲荷	120

Myojo-no-Sugi and Myojo-no-Ike
明星の杉と明星の池

Long, long ago, there lived a high Buddhist priest named Sonkai (尊海), who is known as the person who restored the Kitain Buddhist Temple (喜多院).

One day, he was ordered by the then emperor in Kyoto (京都) to go and preach Buddhism in the Kanto (関東) district. Priest Sonkai immediately left Kyoto and traveled east riding in an ox-drawn carriage. He finally arrived near to Semba (仙波), the area around the Kitain Temple in Kawagoe (川越), when his ox suddenly stopped walking at one end of the bridge over a stream and would not move at all. Then the priest got inspiration from the place and believed in something sacred there. He decided to stay there for a while to investigate.

Later that night, there appeared strange light shining brightly in the nearby pond. In an instant, the light soared up high into the sky, turning the Morning Star, It stayed over an old Japanese cedar tree, and began to twinkle.

"This must surely be a holy place of Buddhism," he thought to himself. Priest Sonkai, researching the place carefully, learned that it was the very place at which great priests of Sempo Sen'nin (仙芳仙人 Hermit Sempo) and Jikaku Daish En'nin (慈覚大師 円仁 Great Buddhist Teacher Jikaku) had once studied and trained themselves a long time before.

In honor of those two saints' great work, Priest Sonkai soon built a temple, and made it the place to lecture on Buddhism.

Because of the legend, people came to call the temple 'Seiya-san (星野山),' meaning 'The Temple Standing on Green Fields under the Morning Star.' The pond was called Myojo-no-Ike (明星の池 = The Pond of the Morning Star), and the cedar tree Myojo-no-Sugi (明星の杉 = The Cedar of the Morning Star).

In order to pass on the legend to the coming generations, a young cedar tree is planted now where the Myojo-no-Sugi cedar tree once stood. It is in the precincts of a small shrine standing in the north corner of the Myojo Parking Lot (明星駐車場) next to Sanmon (山門) main gate of the Kitain Temple.

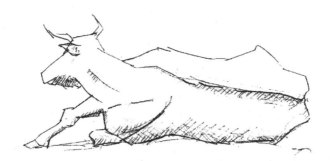

The Main Temple called Cho' on Den
潮 音 殿

The Jie-do Hall (慈恵堂), the main temple building of the Kitain Buddhist Temple (喜多院), has another name of Cho'on-den (潮音殿).

This is the story of why the Jie-do Hall came to be called Cho'on-den.

A long time ago, people, sitting up still in this large quiet main hall and listening very carefully, could hear the sound of the sea. Strange to say, it sounded as if the tide were rising and ebbing, "Za-za-zah, za-za-zah." Surprised to hear such a sound of the tide in this hall, people said to each other, "That sounds just like waves." Nobody knows when, but gradually people came to call the hall 'Cho-on-den,' meaning "The Hall with the Sound of the Sea."

Today, over the entrance of the main temple, there is a wooden plaque with three kanji characters on, which reads Cho-on-den (潮音殿). It was written by Priest Tenkai Sojo (天海僧正 Bishop Tenkai or 慈眼大師 Jigen Daishi, the Great Buddhist Teacher), who was the 27th chief priest at the Kitain Temple.

It is said that the area around the Kitain Temple used to be, as far as people could see, under the vast sea in ancient times, and that people had to use boats wherever they went.

It was Sempo Sen'nin (仙芳仙人), the hermit, who changed a part of the sea into land in order to build a temple here, by asking Ryujin (竜神), the God of the Sea, for help. So a legend goes.

As proof of the fact that the coastline of Tokyo-wan Bay (東京湾) used to be in this neighborhood, there is a historical site of a shell mound called Ko-Semba Kai-zuka Shell Mound (小仙波貝塚) within easy walking distance of the Kitain Temple.

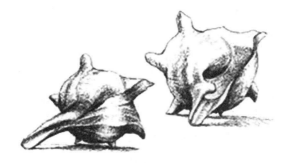

No Bell Ringing at the Kitain Temple (No.1)
山内禁鈴（その一）

It all began in the grounds of the Kitain Buddhist Temple a long time ago. One night a beautiful young woman came to the Kitain Temple and said to the head priest, "Could you do me a favor, sir? I'd like you to stop striking the bell for one hundred days from today on. If you accept my request, I will make the bell sound much more beautiful in return for your kindness."
Saying so, she disappeared somewhere into the darkness of the night.

The priest thought that it would be all right not to strike the bell for only a hundred days if it would help somebody.

Days passed away and on the hundredth night, another beautiful young woman came to the temple and asked a favor of the head priest with tears in her eyes.

"My dear Head Priest, please grant my request for pity's sake. Ring the bell only once tonight, please!" she said.
The priest thought that he had to help her too by ringing the bell only once on the last day of the promised 100 days.

"The first woman would understand my intention if I explain the reason," he thought to himself.

He immediately rang the bell. There went the bell "Gwo-o-ong." It sounded long and beautiful. Then all at once the young woman changed into such a dreadful dragon that no one could look it straight in the face. She gathered winds, rode on the clouds and flew up high into the night sky. The second sound of the bell the priest made sounded dull without reverberations "Gong." No sooner had the loud noise been heard from the south of the temple, than a flash of lightening split the sky, the wind and rain got worse than ever before. The priest began to spin rapidly like a waterwheel - spin, spin, spin, spin. What a surprise! He turned round as many as 99 times! When everything calmed down at last, he came to himself and thought it must have been the curse of the first woman.

Since then, ringing bells, even small ones, has been forbidden in the grounds of the Kitain Temple.

No Bell Ringing at the Kitain Temple(No.2)
山内禁鈴 （その二）

This is what happened in the old days. One day a priest at the Kitain Buddhist Temple went somewhere near Isanuma Swamp (伊 佐 沼) on business. On the way there, he saw a throng of children of the village persecuting a little snake they caught.

The priest said to them, "Now, listen to me, kids. Don't do such a cruel thing to a poor living creature. Please let me have the snake for this." He gave the children some money and brought the snake back to the temple. There he set the snake free in the grounds.

As the years went by, the snake grew big. It went out into the neighboring fields and damaged them. The priest got angry with the snake and said, "I have taken care of you in pity of you. But now I cannot allow you to trouble people by ravaging their fields. From now on, you must stay in the pond in Semba Village (仙波村). Never come out unless I ring for some work I have for you. He confined the snake in the pond.

After that, they decided not to ring bells in the grounds of the temple.

No Bell Ringing at the Kitain Temple
– An Angry Big Snake –
山内禁鈴（怒った大蛇）

Long ago, there was a certain head priest at the Kitain Temple who was truly a snake person. Every day he fed snakes. And each time he gave them food, he made it a rule to ring the bell as a signal. Those snakes always looked forward to hearing the bell ring. Satisfied, they never troubled the priests at Kitain or its neighbors, either. However, the snake-loving head priest was suddenly struck down by illness and finally passed away.

The next priest, who succeeded the late head priest, was said to hate snakes. Even the word of "snake" made him sick and stay in bed. And so, other priests did not ring bells thinking of the head priest, the hater of snakes. The snakes living in the temple grounds, not fed, decreased in number. Some died from hunger, and some moved somewhere else. Only one snake was left at last.

Many years went by. One day, a vendor came to the Kitain Temple. He walked into its grounds ringing a bell. At that moment, a big snake abruptly slithered out. People were so frightened that they ran helter-skelter. It was the only snake that survived. The snake was overjoyed at the sound of a bell and came out expecting to be fed. Learning there was nothing to eat, the snake began to rampage like mad, destroying things in the temple grounds and doing damage even to the houses in the neighborhood.

After that incident, in the precincts of the Kitain Temple, they began to prohibit ringing bells strictly. In addition, they decided to use bells with no clappers in the precincts of the temple.

Three Foxes
三びきのキツネ

Many many years ago, at the Kitain Temple, there lived a virtuous and distinguished Buddhist priest named Tenkai Sojo (天海僧正 Bishop Tenkai).

One day, three young boys came to see Tenkai Sojo and asked him eagerly, "Please allow us to be your disciples, sir. We will do anything patiently."

So Tenkai Sojo allowed them to stay at the temple as training priests. They worked very hard. Those three trainees highly respected Tenkai Sojo, and trained themselves earnestly, watching their teacher's manners and behaviors all the time.

Then one day, something urgent came up in Nikko (日光), and Tenkai Sojo had to go there in a hurry. He went up to the top of the mound in the garden, rang a bell, and flew up high into the sky with magical power. The three boys, watching silently their teacher fly, wanted to fly, too. One boy held a broom in his hand, another held a mortar, and the other a pestle in his hand. All the three tried to fly from the mound as their master did, but did not succeed. Then they tried flying from the top of a tall cedar tree this time. How reckless! They fell directly into the pond down below and died.

When Tenkai Sojo came back, he looked down at the surface of the pond in surprise. There he found the three old foxes floating on the water, with a broom, a mortar and a pestle in their hands respectively.

Tenkai Sojo, feeling pity for them, dedicated a shrine to those three foxes and named it Sanmi Inari (三位稲荷　Three-Fox Shrine).

And so, in the grounds of the Kitain Temple, they prohibited ringing bells. They also decided to put brooms upside down, and to keep mortars and pestles separate.

The 'Tanuki' in the Shape of a Boy
小僧に化けた狸

Long long time ago, there lived in the Kitain Temple a head priest named Jikkai Sojo (実海僧正　Bishop Jikkai). Because he was a man of virtue, many people adored and respected him.

One day, Jikkai Sojo was chanting a sutra in the main hall of the temple, when a strange boy suddenly appeared and said, "My name is Shinsanmi (新三位), sir. Please take me on as a pupil." Then he sat down in the corner of the hall and began to pray together with the bishop.

From that time on, the boy always followed the bishop wherever he went, and listened to him preach people sermons. Coming back to the temple, he cleaned and did the washing every day without fail. At nights, after everybody else fell sound asleep, he studied hard alone.

So the days went by. The boy was never discouraged and never missed doing his work.

One day, however, a sexton, without intention, happened to look into the boy's room. What a surprise! He found a tanuki (狸) raccoon dog sleeping like a log there. The sexton shouted in surprise. The tanuki woke up in astonishment. The tanuki knew that its true character had been found out. So it immediately went to Jikkai Sojo, saying, "I'm a tanuki raccoon dog, sir. I had lived long underneath the floor of Kitain's main hall. Having listened to your sermons, I was deeply moved and wanted to be your disciple to train myself. I have done my best, but now you know what I am. I can't stay here any longer. I will never forget your many kindnesses done to me."

Then the tanuki raccoon dog disappeared under the floor of the

19

main hall.

It is said that there are many big holes under the floor of the Kitain Temple buildings and that they lead in every direction.

The Hawks of Shoromon Gate
鐘楼門の鷹

A number of pigeons are always flying about in the compound of the Kitain Temple. Since pigeons are thought to be messengers of gods, the temple cherishes them, and local people often come and feed them too. So the pigeons, being afraid of nothing in the temple grounds, are playing around and strutting about with a masterful air. But there is one and only place to which pigeons never go near.

One day in the past, a pigeon, unconscious of his carelessness, was playing on the roof of Akamon Gate (赤門 Red Gate = Shoro-mon Gate 鐘楼門 /show-roe-mong/), which had a bell hanging inside. The pigeon began to play tricks as usual. Just then, there was a loud flap of a bird's wings. The pigeon opened his eyes wide in astonishment and saw a hawk glaring at him with piercing eyes. Taken by surprise, he fled in a flurry back to the flock of his friends.

"Never have we heard such a thing!" other pigeons said to each other after listening to his report. So they decided to go to the gate together to see if his story was true. On the red Shoro-mon Gate, they looked over the structure very carefully only to find two wooden carvings of hawks. Then the pigeons felt easy and began to play again without fear.

All of a sudden, the hawks, thought to be wooden carvings, spread their wings and attacked the pigeons.

How terrifying! The pigeons were terrified out of their senses and flew away at full speed toward the main temple.

Since that time, pigeons have never been near to Shoro-mon Gate, they say.

These hawks were reportedly carved by Hidari Jingoro (左甚五郎), a great master sculptor from Hida (飛騨) district.

Pebbles on the Stone Lanterns
石燈ろうの小石

Right next to the Kitain Temple, there are gorgeous red buildings called Toshogu Shrine (東照宮). In its precincts stand several pairs of stone lanterns (石 燈 籠 /ee-she-doe-roe/), all of which have pebbles piled up on them.

In days past, people came here and prayed to the guardian god to help them get rid of troubles or to grant them requests. As people prayed, they quietly and carefully put one pebble upon another on the lanterns. By doing so, strangely enough, all the troubles were eased no matter how difficult they were, and all the wishes were fulfilled as if by miracle. The more pebbles, the more propitious. So people believed, and they competed with each other to make their piles bigger.

The Toshogu Shrine enshrines the spirit of Tokugawa Ieyasu (徳 川 家 康), the original founder of the Tokugawa Shogunate Government. In his childhood, Ieyasu experienced many difficulties. But he overcame them all, and finally he came to rule the whole country as Shogun (将 軍), the ruler. His spirit was believed to have the power to conquer any difficulties and to grant people's wishes. This is why pebbles are piled on the stone lanterns even today.

When Tokugawa Ieyasu died, his body was buried at Mt. Kunozan (久能山), Shizuoka Prefecture (静岡県). One year later, his remains were carried to his final resting place at Nikko (日光), Tochigi Prefecture (栃 木 県). On the way there, Priest Tenkai

Sojo (天海僧正) made the funeral procession stop and stay at the Kitain Temple for four days. He held a solemn Buddhist memorial service for the spirit of Ieyasu. To commemorate this event, Priest Tenkai had this Toshogu Shrine erected in 1633.

These stone lanterns were donated by successive lords of Kawagoe-jo Castle (川越城) during the Edo period. (江戸時代 1603-1868)

Gohyaku Rakan, Five Hundred Rakan Saints
五百羅漢さま

Speaking of Kawagoe, there is a Buddhist temple called the Kitain Temple (喜多院) which everybody visits at least once in their lifetime. The Kitain Temple has a long and distinguished history. It is well known as the temple that has a great number of treasures, many of which are designated as national important cultural properties.

Among the treasures a lot of people love are Gohyaku Rakan (五百羅漢) stone statues. They are the statues placed beside the Sanmon Gate (山門), which represent the 500 disciples of Buddha Sakyamuni (釈迦牟尼). Some are smiling, some are crying, and others are angry. You can also find a statue whispering something to the other. So many statues, so many expressions and gestures.

It is said that a man named Shijo (志誠) started to make these statues a long time ago in 1782, wishing something deep in mind, and that he became sick and died without fulfilling his life desire. So they say that three monks at the Kitain Temple felt pity for him, took over his work, and finished carving over 500 statues. Tradition says that it took them more than 50 years.

Here is a mysterious story about the Gohyaku Rakan statues. If you visit the place all alone without a light in the dead of the night and pat the statues on the heads one by one, you can feel one head warm. Put a mark on it and go back to it next morning, then you will find the face of the statue resembling your parent who passed away.

Dorobo Bashi Bridge
どろぼう橋

Over the moat, at around the back of the Kitain Temple's main hall, there is a bridge that has been called Dorobo Bashi (どろぼう橋), meaning 'The Thief Bridge.'

Here is an old story that tells how the bridge got its name, Dorobo Bashi.

It all happened in the days when the bridge was narrow and made of wood. Thieves and robbers, having committed crimes in the town and been chased by the town police, crossed the bridge and took sanctuary in the grounds of the Kitain Temple to escape capture. In those days, the temple grounds were outside the jurisdiction of the town police.

In the temple, thieves and robbers confessed their sins to Odaishi-sama (お大師様 Great Buddhist Teacher), and threw themselves on his mercy. Even criminals themselves became gentle and obedient in Odaishi-sama's presence, decided to go straight.

That is why people gradually began to call this bridge Dorobo Bashi.

Another story tells us why the bridge came to be called Dorobo Bashi. One day in the past, a thief tried to slip into the temple grounds to steal something, and he, getting into a flurry, dropped into the moat from the bridge.

At that time in the Edo period (江戸時代 1603~1868), the Kitain Temple was in the midst of a thick forest of tall Japanese cedar trees, and the road that led from the Kitain Temple to Kubo-machi

(久保町) neighborhood was as dark as night even in the daytime. It was said that once clouds hung low over Semba-yama (仙波山) hill, it certainly started to rain.

Enoki Inari
榎の木稲荷

A long time ago, in the Kitain Temple, lived a clever white fox, which was very good at transforming itself into a man. But one day, at last, it was found out what it really was. And it decided to ask the temple to give him a leave and was to leave the temple. Then the white fox went to see the head priest, Sonkai Sojo (尊海僧正 Bishop Sonkai), and said that it had to leave the temple. The fox thanked him for his favor and proffered to show him one thing as a token of its gratitude.

"Your Reverence, I will turn myself into Buddha Sakyamuni (釈迦牟尼、釈迦 the founder of Buddhism) and show you how he preached people over 2500 years ago. But, sir, you certainly shouldn't utter even a single word whatever happens during my transformation. Could you promise, sir?"

Sonkai Sojo promised faithfully to keep silent, thinking it would be very grateful to be able to see such a venerable person even in a dream. When what the white fox promised was really displayed before his very eyes, however, Sonkai Sojo, though great, was overjoyed and murmured words unconsciously.

"Oh, my! Thank Buddha! 南無阿弥陀仏 /nah-moo-ah-mee-dah-boo-tsoo/ (I shall follow Amida Buddha.)"

The next moment, the figure of Buddha Sakyamuni vanished from sight and the fox, which was practicing magic at the top of a tall enoki (榎) hackberry tree fell head over heels onto the ground and died.

Sonkai Sojo, feeling very sorry and pity for the white fox, buried its body with respect at the foot of the enoki tree and built a small shrine for it.

It is, they say, this Enoki Inari Shrine (榎の木稲荷 Hackberry Fox Shrine) that now stands at the foot of the big enoki tree.

Bottomless Hole
底なしの穴

Right in front of the sanmon front gate (山門) of the Kitain Temple, there is a shrine called Hie Jinja Shrine (日枝神社). The main shrine building is designated as a national important cultural property. In its small precincts, there used to be a deep, deep hole which people called 'Bottomless Hole (底なしの穴)' from olden times. The hole was much too deep for people to see the bottom.

One day, some people in the neighborhood got together and were talking to each other by the hole.

"I want to know how deep on earth this hole is."

"Why don't we throw in something on trial?"

So, they threw a pan into the hole, expecting to hear it drop onto the bottom. They were all ears but not a sound was heard.

"Now, let's try again with some other things!" Then they, one after another, threw in a wooden bowl, a pair of geta (下駄) wooden clogs, and so on. But none of them made any sound at all.

"What in the world is this hole like down there?"

They were looking down into the deep hole wondering why.

Then there came a man from the direction of Futago Ike Pond (双子池 Pond of Twins), and said, "Say, guys! Lots of things are floating on the pond down there."

So they immediately walked down to the pond to find all the things which they had thrown into the bottomless hole were now floating there. They were once again very surprised at this mysterious hole and began to call it Bottomless Hole.

Futago Ike Pond is located about 500 meters away from Hie Jinja shrine and is also called 'Dragon Pond' or 'Benten Pond (弁天池 Pond of the Goddess of Music)'. There is a legend about this pond which tells that Sempo Sen'nin, a saint, enshrined a dragon into it in ancient times.

The Unearthly Cedar Tree
お化け杉

Within a few minutes' walk of the Kitain temple's main gate, there used to be a temple called Enma-do (閻魔堂 the Temple for the Judge of Hell).

In the compound of Enma-do, there was once a towering old cedar tree called Jamon Sugi (蛇紋杉 the Snakeskin- Patterned Cedar). The tree is said to have been very old and to have been covered with the bark which looked like the striped pattern of snakeskin. Because of its creepy patterned bark, people felt uneasy with the tree.

"Say, guys! Why don't we venture to hew it down?" said somebody. Then all agreed and decided to cut it down.
A number of people began to give it cuts with broadaxes. They were cutting, "Chop! Chop! Chop!"
How creepy! Blood started to trickle down from the cut in the trunk. People were so scared at the terrible sight that they ran back home. In a little while, those who tried to cut it down began to suffer from serious illness.

And what was even stranger, when the cedar tree was seen from the distance, it looked as if it were a pine tree.
"Why! I wonder if there is such a big pine tree in the compound of the Enma-do temple."
All the people, seeing the tree from the distance, said to each other. Feeling puzzled, they went near to the tree to have a close look at it. It was certainly a cedar tree. Surprised, they went back to where they had been to look at it again. From that place,

they again found a pine tree without a doubt. Not knowing why it was, they were very scared of the cedar tree and began to call it 'The Blood Dripping Cedar' or 'The Weird Cedar.'

But the cedar tree was all gone. We cannot find any trace of it now.

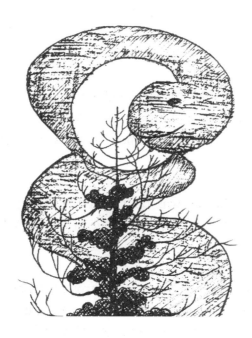

Biwa Bashi Bridge
琵琶橋

This is a story in the old days. One day, Sonkai Sojo (尊 海 僧 正 Bishop Sonkai), who is said to have been the restorer of the Kitain Buddhist Temple, went out to somewhere in the distance attended by his disciples. But on their way back, they got lost. When they came to a stream, they found it impossible for them to wade across it because it was brimming with water. Even very clever Sonkai Sojo was at a loss what to do, when there came a blind 'biwa hoshi (琵 琶 法 師 a priest who chants tales playing the musical instrument of lute).'

Sonkai Sojo's disciples told him that they had got lost and asked him the way back to the temple.

"Ah, it's just too bad. All right, then. Let me help you," said the blind 'biwa hoshi'. And then he laid the biwa (琵琶 lute) that he had across the stream.

"There, you can cross here. Go ahead, please," he said.
And Sonkai Sojo and his disciples could safely cross the stream and stand on the other side. They finally went back to the Kitain Temple.

Afterwards, a bridge was built over the stream, and was called Semba Biwa Bashi, or the Lute Bridge of Semba Village.

A little bird says that if you look through under the bridge, you can see through. But if you try to walk through under the bridge, you will be out of sight when you go halfway. It is also said that if you turn around three times on the bridge, you will disappear in the same way.

Kiri-fuki-no Ido
霧吹きの井戸

In the northeast corner of the Kawagoe-jo Castle (川越城) grounds, there used to be an old well walled with stones. It was called 'Kiri-fuki no Ido (霧吹きの井戸)', meaning 'The Well That Makes Fog.'

A long time ago, Kawagoe-jo Castle was the stage where many wars and battles were done. This well in the castle grounds was usually kept covered in peacetime. But when a battle broke out and the castle was in danger attacked by the enemy, they immediately took the lid off the well and kept its mouth wide open. Then strangely enough, volumes of dense fog began to flow out of the well and lay all around. The heavy fog soon covered the castle and hid it completely. The castle having gone out of the sight suddenly, the enemy could not do other than withdraw in the thick fog.

After the enemy was gone, the fog was also gone and the fine castle came in sight again, and everything reverted to normal.

And so, Kawagoe-jo Castle was also called 'Kiri-Gakure Jo (霧隠城 The Castle Hidden by the fog).

The Sacrifice of a Maiden
人身御供

The area where Kawagoe-jo Castle (川越城) once stood had been marshy land called 'Nanatsu Gama' (七ツ釜 The Seven Ponds). And so, people met many difficulties in building a castle on such soft and muddy ground.

Long ago, warlords Ota Doshin (太田道真) and Ota Dokan (太田道灌), father and son, were building a huge mound of earth to construct Kawagoe-jo Castle. However, they were not successful in spite of their hard work, and were at a loss what to do.

One night, the Ryujin Dragon God (竜神), the Spirit of the Ponds, appeared in Doshin's dream and said, "Offer me the person, as a sacrifice, whom you will see first tomorrow morning, then your desire of raising a castle shall be accomplished."

In order to build a castle, Doshin unwillingly made up his mind to follow Ryujin God's divine message.

Then the next morning came. To his surprise, it was his own daughter who was the first to come and see him. Doshin was astonished and confused indeed. He, however, resigned himself to his fate and told her all about the dream.

"Actually, dear Father, I had the same dream as you did. This is, I believe, the Ryujin God's will. I am quite ready for being a sacrifice if I can be much help to people," said his daughter.

Ignoring everybody's attempt to restrain her, she threw herself into one of the ponds and offered herself to Ryujin, the Spirit of the Ponds.

By virtue of this noble sacrifice, Kawagoe-jo Castle was finally completed. It was in the first year of Choroku (長禄元年 1457) of the Muromachi Period (室町時代), they say.

Kataha-no Ashi
片葉の葦

A long time ago, there lived a young princess in Kawagoe-jo Castle. One night, when the castle was attacked and captured by the enemy, the princess had a narrow escape from the castle taken by her old nanny. They ran away into the marshland, not far away from the castle, and finally came to the swampy land, near to Ukishima Jinja shrine (浮島神社). The place was thickly covered with tall reeds and called Nanatsu Gama (七つ釜), meaning the Seven Ponds. Just at that time, the princess slipped into one of the seven ponds by mistake.

"Oh, no! Help! Somebody! Help my princess!" the nanny screamed for help, forgetting that they were running away behind the enemy's back. But nobody came to help them. The old nanny tried and tired to help the princess with all her might, but could not make it anyway.

Coming up and going down in the water, the princess was just struggling. She reached out for something to hold on to, and finally clung to the blades, or long and flat leaves of a reed nearby. She desperately tried to get out of the water, but the long and thin blades were quite easily ripped off.

The poor little princess, still holding the blades of a reed in her hand, sank to the bottom of the pond. She died a tragic death.

Thereafter, all the reeds growing around the Nanatsu Gama ponds are the ones called Kataha-no-Ashi, meaning ' a reed whose blades grow only on one side of its stalk,' they say.

Pebble-Throwing Service at the Yona-gawa River
よな川の小石供養

Long ago, there lived in the village of Yoshino (芳 野), northeast of Kawagoe, a young girl named Oyone. Oyone was the daughter of the head of the village, and she was beautiful and good-natured.

One day, when the lord of Kawagoe-jo Castle came to the village for falconry, kosho(小 姓) or a young handsome boy attendant, who served the lord being close at hand all the time, saw Oyone and fell in love with her at first sight. After meeting several times, he took her for his wife.

Although the two loved each other, Oyone had a hard time living in a strict samurai family. Moreover, her mother-in-law was a difficult person to get along well with, and she was even harder on Oyone especially after her son had gone to work.

One day, Oyone was putting back the precious plates into the chest, which her husband had gratefully received from the lord. Accidentally she broke one of them. After that her mother-in-law treated her even worse than before. Oyone could not endure it any longer and left the house. But, with no one to turn to, she committed suicide by throwing herself into the river.

Her husband, learning about this, went nearly mad with grief. He went to the river and called out, "Oyone, my love! Oyone!" day after day. Then the tiny bubbles came up from the bottom of the river as if she were replying, "I'm down here, dear." Not being able to endure great deal of grief any longer, he also threw himself into the river and died at last.

Afterwards, when people passed by the river, moved by this story, they would pick up some pebbles and throw them into the water to offer their sympathy. Then numerous bubbles rose from the bottom as if in answer to this.

So people called the river Oyone-gawa (およね川 the River Oyone), and as the years went by, it came to be called the Yona-gawa (よな川 the River Yona).

Tenjin Mitarashi－no Seisui
天神洗足の井水

 In the old days, warlords of Ota Doshin (太田道真) and Dokan (道 灌), father and son, were planning to construct Kawagoe-jo Castle (川越城). In order to lead water to the moats of the castle, they were looking for the source of water. Day after day, they walked up and down seeking for the good springs, but they were not successful in finding any particular spot and were at a loss.

One day, Dokan was on an everyday search expecting to find the source of water, mumbling "Where on earth can I get water?" Just as he was passing by the tall cedar tree called Hatukari-no Sugi (初雁の杉 The Cedar of the First Wild Geese To Come), he unexpectedly saw an old man soaking his feet in well water and washing them with it. Dokan stopped and looked at the water carefully to find it was a fountain from which water was gushing out. Dokan told the old man about building a castle with moats and asked for his help, then the old man nodded and led Dokan to the springs which was brimming with water and looked inexhaustible.

According to their wishes, Doshin and Dokan finally completed Kawagoe-jo Castle, the castle invulnerable to attack.
Dokan wanted to express his sincere thanks to the old man and searched for him far and wide. But he could not find him anyway.

Then an idea came across his mind. He was sure that the old man was certainly the incarnation of Tenjin God (天神) that they always believed in. And so he named the well water 'Tenjin Mitarashi-no Seisui (天神洗足の井水 The Well Water With Which

Tenjin God Washed His Feet) to honor the God. He wanted the well and its name to be remembered long even in days to come.

The well is said to have been somewhere in the castle grounds. But today nobody knows where it was really located. It might have possibly been somewhere around Miyoshino Tenjin Jinja shrine (三芳野神社) or somewhere else, they say.

Hatsukari-no Sugi
初雁の杉

The Miyoshino Jinja Shrine (三芳野神社), which is said to have been the birthplace of the nursery rhyme of 'Toryanse (とうりゃんせ / toh-ryang-say/ You may pass.), was originally founded in the Heian Period (平安時代 794-1192), they say. Also, it was located in the castle grounds and was called 'Tenjin-jinja shrine in the Castle grounds (お城の天神さま).'

At the back of the shrine, there used to be an absolutely marvelous Japanese cedar tree. It was familiarly called by people 'Hatsukari-no-Sugi (初雁の杉 The Cedar Tree of the First Wild Geese).

In the old days, when the wild geese from the northern skies flew over to Kawagoe, they honked three times over the cedar tree, and circled around three times over it. They then flew south. This was surely performed every year without fail.

That is why people began to call Kawagoe-jo Castle (川越城) Hatsukari-jo (初雁城 Castle of the First Wild Geese). The area around the castle was called Miyoshino (三芳野) and was written about in tanka (短歌) poems of thirty-one syllables. There are two poems in the book called "Ise Monogatari (伊勢物語", or "The Story of Ise" — Story with Poems) wtitten in the Heian Period.

Earnestly honks the poor wild goose
Over the rice paddies of Tanomu (田面)
In the beautiful land of Miyosino (三芳野)

Yearning to be close to you.

三芳野の　田面の雁は　ひたぶるに
/mee-yoh-she-no-no tah-no-moo-no kahree-wah-he-tah-boo-roo-nee/
君が方にぞよると　鳴くなる
/kee-mee-gah-kah-tah-nee-zoh yoh-roo-toh nah-coo-nah-roo/

The wild goose in Miyosino may yearn blind
Longing to be perched on my shoulder
Yet as the time grows older
The wild goose of Tanomu shall be out of my mind.

わが方によると　なくなる三芳野の
/wah-gah-kah-tah-nee yoh-roo-toh nah-coo-nah-roo mee yoh-shc-no-no
田面の雁を　いつかわすれむ
/tah-no-moo-no-kahree-woh ee-tsoo-kah wah-sue-ren

The Noise of Running Horses in the Castle
城中蹄の音

The first lord of Kawagoe-jo Castle (川 越 城) at the very beginning of the Edo Period (江 戸 時 代 1603-1868) was Sakai Kawachi-no-kami Shigetada, Lord of Kawachi (酒井河内守重忠), who was well known as the brave and strong warrior in the whole wide country.

When the night grew old, and when everybody fell fast asleep, mysteriously the battle cry of warriors, whooshes of arrows and the noise of dashing horses could be heard from nowhere in the castle. There were such enigmatic happenings every night. Lord Sakai became afraid, though he was the brave and strong warrior. So he decided to consult a fortuneteller. Then the fortuneteller told that there was a picture of war inside the castle, which asked for trouble. Lord Sakai immediately ordered his men to search for it in the treasury. They found a set of folding screens that depicted the Night Raid at Horikawa (堀川夜討) as the fortuneteller told. He learned that those screens had caused trouble, so he decided to separate them. He contributed one half to the Yojuin Temple (養寿院) where he always worshipped.

Then strangely enough, from that night on, no strange noises of war cry, no whooshes or no hooves were heard. He came to feel easy enough to sleep in peace.

This folding screen is said to be treasured at the Yojuin Temple even today.

The Gravestone of Mushi-kui Yakko
虫食い奴の墓

On the street where kurazukuri (蔵造り the clay-walled fireproof house) houses stand in a row, there is an old temple named Jinenzan Hozenji (自然山法善寺). On the right side, after passing through the sanmon gate (山門 the front gate) of the temple, there stands a stone statue of a man in samurai attire, sitting on what looks like a sake barrel. The local people call the statue 'Mushi-kui Yakko-no Haka (虫食い奴の墓 The Gravestone of the Bug-Eating Yakko Servant).

There was once a lord of Kawagoe-han Clan (川越藩) whose name was Matsudaira Nobutsuna (松平信綱). Among his men, there was a samurai warrior named Ishikawa Sakuemon (石川作右衛門), whom Segawa Kaemon (瀬川嘉右衛門), the man represented in this statue, served as a lance carrier called yakko (奴).

The yakko servant perfectly did what his master ordered him, serving him faithfully and earnestly. The yakko loved sake very much and drank sake like a fish without missing a single day. He was not only a heavy drinker but a man of odd taste. What he liked as a side dish for sake were mice, snakes, and even bugs. He liked especially rotten meat. He was such a strange man that he lived alone with no family to live with. So he built his own gravestone in the grounds of the Hozenji temple while he was alive.

The gravestone created a sensation throughout the castle town of Kawagoe, and many people visited it one after another. After a while, Kaemon died, but the gravestone of "a yakko servant who ate bugs (虫食い奴)" became more and more popular, and people came even a long way to see it.

The present gravestone is said to be the second one.

The Story of the Bell at the Time Bell Tower
時の鐘のはなし

The row of kurazukuri (蔵造り thickly daubed fireproof house) houses, and the Toki-no-Kane Time Bell Tower (時の鐘) will easily catch your eye while you are strolling around in the old town of Kawagoe. Today this bell charms the people of Kawagoe with its gentle sound, and they take pride in it.

Now here is an old story about a bell. The bell was called 'Chokyu-no Ne (長久の音),' or 'Everlasting Sound' and was loved by the ninth lord of Kawagoe-jo Castle, Akimoto Takatomo (秋元喬知).

When he was to be transferred from his former domain in Koshu Yamura (甲州谷村), Yamanashi Prefecture (山梨県), to Kawagoe, he reluctantly decided to leave his favorite bell behind because it was too heavy to carry a long way. But on the night before his departure, the bell hung in the bell tower dropped onto the ground. They wondered why, and after checking it up, they found that the dragon-shaped cannon of the bell was broken. They repaired it right away and hung it. But soon the cannon broke and the bell dropped again. Every time they repaired it, the result was the same. Scared of strange happenings, the followers consulted with Lord Akimoto about the bell. He thought that the bell was complaining about the pain of parting and appealing to them to take it to Kawagoe with them. So they decided to carry it in cooperation with each other. Strange to say, on their way to Kawagoe, they did not feel the weight of the bell at all, and besides no one was injured. They had no difficulty arriving in Kawagoe. And the bell was hung in the Toki-no-Kane, the Time Bell Tower.

49

When Lord Akimoto was transferred to Dewa-no-kuni (出羽の国), Yamagata Prefecture, later, he took with him the bell called 'Chokyuu-no-Ne (長久の音)' to his new domain again, they say.

The Bell at the Renkei-ji Temple
蓮馨寺の鐘

The Renkei-ji Temple (蓮馨寺) in Kawagoe City is popularly known as 'Donryu-sama (呑竜さま Dear Priest Donryu 1556~1623), or Kosodate-no-Kami (子育ての神 the God of Raising Children).

This temple was one of the 18 Priests' Schools of the Jodo-shu Sect of Buddhism (浄土宗関東十八檀林) in the Kanto district (関東地方).

At the request of Renkei-ni (蓮 馨 尼 Nun Renkei), mother of Daidoji Suruga-no-kami Masashige (大道寺駿河守正繁 Daidoji Masashige, Lord of Suruga), this temple was founded by great priest Kan'yo Shonin (感誉上人) late in the Muromachi period (室町時代 1335-1563).

Long, long ago, there was a whopping fire in the town of Kawagoe, and a big section of it was destroyed. Renkei-ji temple caught fire and all the buildings of the temple burned up. When the blazing flames were just about to catch the bell tower, one priest dashed up the bell tower and began to strike the bell passionately, "Gwo-o-ong, gwo-o-ong, ⋯" There was virtually a sea of flames surrounding the bell tower. Everybody there shouted to the priest, "Run away quick, please! The fire won't go out!"

Not fazed by the flames at all, he kept on striking the bell. It seemed that the fire hesitated at the worthy and devoted behavior of the priest, and did not touch the bell tower. Far from it, it seemed that the fire kept away from the bell tower. Though the force of the fire died down after a while, the town was destroyed completely. People saw only the bell tower of Renkei-ji temple rising from ruins of the fire. They did not see the priest who was striking the bell.

Later on, people knew without a doubt that the priest was really the 'Donryu-sama,' and were most grateful to him once again.

Even today, at the temple festival of Donryu-sama held on the eighth of every month, its grounds are crowded with lots of people.

Yukizuka Inari Fox Shrine
雪塚稲荷

On a snowy winter night, in the far past, a snow-white fox strayed into the street in Minami-machi neighborhood (南町 now Saiwai-cho 幸町), yelping "Koh-oh-ong! Koh-oh-ong!" Catching sight of the white fox, some young men rushed out into the snow-covered street and ran after the fox, hitting it with sticks in their hands. Chased by madding youngsters, even a quick white fox could not make good its escape. It was driven into a dark alley and beaten to death at last.

Days passed. One day, those who struck the fox to death began to fall on evil days. They began to suffer from an epidemic disease one after another, and their houses were attacked by big fire balls in the dead of the night. The people in the neighborhood were very much afraid and thought that the spirit of that snow-white fox must have been cursing them.

And so, in the grounds of the nearby Choki-in temple (長喜院), they built a small shrine and enshrined the soul of the snow-white fox as the guardian deity of the neighborhood. After that, both an epidemic disease and fire balls were all gone.

In memory of that snowy night, they named the shrine 'Yukizuka Inari (雪塚稲荷),' meaning 'The Fox Shrine on the Snow-covered Mound,' and set up its annual festival on the 12th of April.

Yukizuka Inari Shrine is said to be miraculously responsive to prayers wishing for thriving business, and it constantly attracts many worshippers even from far away.

Kubo Inari Shrine
くぼ稲荷

Since there are two very tall old gingko trees in the precincts, Kubo Inari Shrine (くぼ稲荷) in Matsue-cho neighborhood (松江町) is commonly called 'Icho Kubo (銀杏くぼ Kubo Inari with Gingko Trees). It is also called 'Shusse Inari (出世稲荷 Success Inari Shrine).

It happened a long time ago. Once there was a fishmonger who had a firm belief in the God of Kubo Inari. One day he went to a nearby town of Okegawa (桶川) on business, but he had to stay there overnight because it became late at night. He went to bed after readying himself to leave at the break of dawn the next day; for he had some work to do in Kawagoe early in the morning. At midnight, however, a fox appeared in his dream and delivered the message to him, "If you leave here before dawn, evil will surely fall on you."

So the fishmonger leisurely waited for the sun to climb the sky and started a little after noon. Then on the way back to Kawagoe, he came to a place where a crowd of people gathered and talked loudly to each other. He learned that it was the very spot that a young girl had been attacked by a pack of wolves. He shivered with fright and thought that he himself must have been attacked by the wolves if he had started before dawn. He also thought that the fox must have brought him the voice of the God of Kubo Inari Shrine.

He was most grateful to the God and hurried back home. He believed in the God more and more faithfully than ever before and his business prospered and prospered. As a result, he was able to have a bigger store.

So the shrine came to be called 'Shusse Inari (出 世 稲 荷),' or Success Inari Shrine.

It is said that when you make a wish to the God of Kubo Inari, you have to say, "My dearest Inari-san, please help me succeed in life, and I will get you a good wife for your kindness." And you have to offer ema (絵馬 a wooden prayer tablet) with a picture of a young beautiful woman on or a doll of a young beautiful woman.

The Set of Three Images of Jizo Buddha
日ぎり三体地蔵さん

The small fine Jizo-do (地蔵堂) temple stands in the grounds of the Saiun-ji Temple (西雲寺) in Shintomi-cho neighborhood (新富町). In the Jizo-do temple, three little wooden images of Jizo Buddha (地蔵) are enshrined. All of them look different from each other. The origin of these three images is as follows: One stick is unsteady to stand, but three sticks can stand firmly when they are put together, they say. It is said that they symbolize the 'Tristar' in the heavens (the Orion).

To begin with, there is a story which tells why these three Jizo images are niched in this Jizo-do temple at the Saiun-ji Temple.

Once upon a time, a certain lord of Aizu Wakamatsu (会 津 若 松), Fukushima Prefecture (福島県) was sleeping, when there appeared Jizo Buddha in his dream. "Dig me up. I'm buried in the muddy pool with reeds," said Jizo Buddha. The lord soon dug the three images out of mud and enshrined them in the temple named Saiko-ji Temple (西光寺). Then a certain high priest made replicas of them and pilgrimaged across the country carrying them on his back. He finally came to Kawagoe and enshrined them in the Saiun-ji Temple, they say.

People believe that these Jizo images work wonders especially on patients suffering with smallpox. When you make a wish, you get some of the salt and hemp rope kept in Jizo-do temple, and bring them home. Then twist the rope around your neck, drink the salt, and you will wonderfully recover.
In recognition of their help, people offered salt and hemp rope

56

double what they got from Jizo-do temple, people say.

●日ぎり地蔵 (日限地蔵尊 /he-gee-ree jee-zoh-song/)
On special days of 3rd, 5th, 7th, 13th, 15th, 17th, 23rd, 25th, 27th of the month, especially, Jizo Buddha wished for peace to people, cured serious diseases and gave happiness to the poor.

Ocha Kanbo
お茶かんぼう

A long time ago, the beautiful green countryside of Kawagoe was a good place for hunting. After Tokugawa Ieyasu (徳川家康) established in Edo (江戸 now Tokyo 東京) the Tokugawa Bakufu (徳川幕府 the feudal military government of the Tokugawa Family 1603-1868), he often came to Kawagoe area to enjoy falconry, or hunting with hawks.

One day, on his way back from hunting in the fields around the Town of Kawagoe, he arrived somewhere on the Akamagawa River (赤間川), when he felt thirsty and looked for good water to drink. Then he saw a small shabby temple in the woods.

"Oh, how lucky I am to find a temple!" he thought and visited it at once. The priest at the temple was astonished to see the shogun right in front of him. He soon served a cup of hot tea to Shogun Ieyasu (将 軍 家 康) respectfully. Even the shogun, the powerful ruler of the whole country, was so much pleased with a cup of tea. He felt that the tea relieved his fatigue completely and thanked the priest for it.

As his gratitude, he gave an official name of Kansaizan Jurenji (干菜山十連寺) to the temple and decided to donate a piece of land to it as well. When Ieyasu thought that he should write 'shuin-jo (朱印状 the Shogun's official document with red seal on),' he found that he had no such paper with him because he was on a hunting tour. So he took a pocket tissue out of his bosom and wrote his words on it instead.

The temple is said to have kept the tissue for a long time, calling it 'Shogun Ieyasu's Tissue as an Shuin-jo Official Document.'

However, the temple named Kansaizan Jurenji does not exist today.

　There is a place called 'Gongen-zuka (権現塚 The Memorial of Shogun Ieyasu)' or 'Ocha-yu-zuka (お茶湯塚 The Memorial of Water for Shogun's Tea). Some people suppose that it is the place where the temple once stood.

The Tale of Go-no Kami
五の神のはなし

One day, a long time ago, the lord of Kawagoe-han Clan (川越藩) surveyed the farmland strictly, suspecting that the rice paddies unregistered to evade taxes might have existed in and around Ishida-hongo Village (石田本郷). The Lord's men were going to make a survey on pieces of detached land lying between the villages of Ishida-hongo and Yanaka (谷中).

Five peasants living in Ishida-hongo Village, however, made a desperate appeal to the government officials for mercy. They threw themselves to the ground and begged earnestly, "The rivers around here are often flooded by heavy rainstorms, and the rice crop is badly damaged each time. So we fall in great difficulty to pay our land tax with rice. In addition, when the crops failed because of a long spell of dry weather, or when we suffer from famine, we have supplemented with the crop from those detached fields. So, could you please give us mercy by closing your eyes to them in the 'kenchi (検地 official land survey)' ?"

The officials from the Kawagoe-han Clan (川越藩), however, would never accept their request. "If we should make an exception for Ishida-hongo Village, it would be a bad example to other villages," they thought to themselves.

"Nonsense! That's out of the question! You, five! We order you five to get out of this village right away." The officials decided the punishment on the spot, and the five peasants were banished out of the village.

Afterwards, the survey on detached land became less strict, as the officials might have admitted that there had been some truth in what the five peasants had claimed.

So as not to forget those five men of courage, the villagers built a small shrine and worshipped it as 'Go-no-Kami Myojin (五の神明神 The Myojin Shrine for the Five Gods).' The villagers handed down those detached fields, which those five had saved for the village, calling them 'Go-no-Kami,' and never forgot the precious deed done by the five brave peasants.

Gigantic Snakes in Koike Ponds
小池の大蛇

A long time ago, the area around Kita-tajima Village (北田島) used to be a marshland and there were many ponds. It is said that some of those ponds were linked with now existing Isanuma Pond (伊佐沼). In the marshland, there were two deepest ponds. Strangely, no matter how long the drought lasted, these ponds never dried up. From these ponds water was always welling up. So the villagers called them 'Koike (小池 The Little Ponds) and treasured them.

One day, some neighborhood children were playing with water at the side of the ponds. Accidentally one of them fell into the water and was almost drowned, when two gigantic snakes suddenly appeared out of the water and saved the drowning kid. After that, slowly and calmly they went away.

Soon the rumor spread all around. People began to say, "If we pray to the Snakes, the Spirit of the Ponds, they will make it rain in a drought and protect the village from a flood disaster." And so, there came many people continuously and threw offerings into the Ponds and prayed.

Those two gigantic snakes were very friendly with each other and were often seen to go out together. Though they were worshipped as the guardian gods of the village, they might have taken ill and died too easily.

The people in the village really felt pity for the Snakes, building two small shrines and naming them 'Shinmei Shrines (神明社).' One is nowadays worshipped as a private shrine of a family. The other standing in the midst of the rice fields is still visited by the villagers.

In addition, some families are said to keep the Snakes' teeth as family treasures.

Muddy-footed Jizo-san
どろ足の地蔵さん

In the small shrine called Jizo-do（地蔵堂）, at Orito of Ishida-hongo Village（石田本郷）, stands a peculiar stone image of Jizo Buddha（地蔵）. It is called Takaki Jizo（田掻き地蔵 Jizo Buddha who plowed rice paddies) or Hanatori Jizo（鼻取り地蔵 Jizo Buddha who led a horse).

A long time ago, as the rice planting season was drawing near, farmers got ready to plow paddies, leading water into the paddies and taking out horses. But a farmer living at Orito（折戸）was in trouble with nobody to help him.

There appeared a vigorous young man and said, "Hello, there, old man! Let me be your plowboy and lead your horse if it is all right with you."

The young man soon started to plow the fields leading the horse very skillfully. He did the work so cleverly and neatly that he finished the work in the twinkling of an eye. The old farmer was surprised to see the young man work. He looked at the finely finished paddies admiringly for some time. Wanting to say 'thank you' to the young man, he looked back. But there was nobody there.

"Well, well, well⋯ How kind a young man at this busy season! Where on earth he is from, I wonder⋯"

He followed the muddy footprints the young man left. What a surprise! They led him to the Jizo-do shrine at the edge of his village. And when he looked inside at the image of Jizo Buddha carefully, he found Jizo's feet dirty with mud.

"Oh, my Jizo! Now I know that young man was in fact this Jizo-san." So he thanked the Jizo Buddha image for his help once again. He was said to honor and cherish this stone image of Jizo more than ever.

Funa-zuka
船塚

In the area on the Iruma-gawa River (入間川), which is a part of Kami-Oibukuro (上老袋) of Yoshino Village (芳野), there is a kofun (古墳 tumulus) assumed to have been built in the late 6th century.

The River Iruma-gawa used to be very wild and was often flooded with the heavy rain. It burst the banks easily and flowed into the village. So the villagers always had a hell of a time.

One day in the past, there was a flood. The flood washed away houses and caused extensive damage to the village. Some people who were looking for the refuge in boats evacuated to a wooded mound. On the mound they underwent hardship, staving off hunger by eating only a little food they had, and had a narrow escape.

After that, people began to call the mound 'Funa-zuka (船塚 The Mound of Boat). And they learned that it had been an ancient tomb and dug the ground. A lot of artifacts such as earthenware, stone coffin and haniwa (埴輪 earthen figures to decorate and guard the burial mound) were excavated. But since it had been the tomb of somebody in power, those who dug up began to suffer a serious illness. People were so superstitious that they would not go near to it, because they believed that it would take terrible revenge on anyone who just touched it.

Since the area stretching from Kami-Oibukuro over to Furuya Village (古 谷) used to be marshes, people in ancient times are said to have been fishing using dugout canoes.

In fact, dugout canoes assumed to have been made in the late Jomon Period (縄文時代 10,000 BC~300BC) were found and unearthed.

66

One of them was found in the left bank of the Iruma-gawa River, the point a little above the Iruma Ohashi Bridge (入間大橋) at Oibukuro (老袋). The other was found in Ishida-hongo (石田本郷).

One of them is stored in Honmaru Goten (本丸御殿 the main entrance hall of the innermost quarter of the castle).

* The dugout canoe (丸木舟), which was excavated in Oibukuro and is thought to be 3,000 years old, has been displayed in the City Museum since 1990.

Fox at the Zenchu-ji Temple
善仲寺のキツネ

This is an old story. The place around the Zenchuji Temple (善仲寺) is said to have been a forest where a lot of plants had grown so thick that it had been very dark and lonely even during the day. It was the home to some kinds of herons. There also lived in the forest a mischievous fox from olden times.

Near the temple there was an old woman living alone. Although her better half had been dead for a long time, she liked weaving so much that she did not feel lonely at all. One night, she was weaving at a late hour as usual, with her weaving machine making a regular sound, "Zoot-tong-tong! Zoot-tong-tong!"

Suddenly there was a knock at the front door. She hurried to the door and opened it, but she could not find anybody there. Only the wind was blowing.

"It must have been the wind that made a knocking sound," she thought, and resumed weaving.

"Zoot-tong-tong! Zoot-tong-tong!" There came a noise from outside this time. It sounded just like her weaving machine.

"Oh, I bet it's the fox," the old woman thought to herself. Very quietly she opened the koshido (格子戸 the sliding latticed window door) and looked out of it. There! As she had expected, there was an old fox standing on forefeet and tapping on the door with its thick tail. Holding a broomstick in her hand, the old widow opened the front door quickly.

"You, wicked fox! Now I know!" she shouted at the fox. Taken by surprise, even a malicious fox ran away helter-skelter toward the Zenchuji Temple.

The fox, detected tricking, never played a trick on people again, they say.

Otoka-sama in Furuya Village
古谷のオトウカさま

In Konakai (小中居) of Furuya Village (古谷), there is a slightly swelling hillock in a certain spread of rice paddies. This is the shrine called Tsukada Inari Fox Shrine (塚田稲荷), and the local people affectionately call the deity 'Otoka-sama (オトウカさま 'otoka' is another name for a fox).

There lived an old man known as a hard worker in a neighboring village of Numabata (沼端). One day he left home early in the morning to join in the celebration in the nearby village of Kugedo (久下戸). He enjoyed chatting with the folks there all day. By the time he started for home, it had already got dark with the moon shining overhead.

He was approaching Tsukada Inari Shrine carrying many token gifts. Just then he saw a young woman standing ahead of him. When he stole a glance at her by the moonlight, he found she looked very beautiful even in the dark.

"Oh, my! What a beautiful woman!" he said to himself, looking admiringly at her. After a while, when the moon disappeared behind the clouds, he came to himself. The girl had already disappeared. All the food in a chip box given as a present was all gone too.

Otoka-sama, the fox had changed itself into a beautiful young woman and played a trick on him.

The old man very much regretted having been tricked by the fox.

Horo Matsuri and Shishi-Gashira
ほろ祭りと獅子頭

On the riverside of the Arakawa (荒川), in Furuya Village (古谷), there is an old shrine of the Furuoya Hachiman Jinja shrine (古尾谷八幡神社). Its foundation can be traced back to the Heian Period (平安時代 794-1192). The shrine's festival called 'Horo-kake Matsuri (ほろかけ祭り)' is held on September 15th every year. This festival is said to have a long history and to be based on the ceremony to celebrate the young boys' coming of age (at the age of 12 to 16). And only the family's firstborn son has the right to be celebrated in this ceremony and to join the parishioners' society.

'Horo (ほろ = 母衣)' is a large piece of cloth like a big balloon worn by a warrior on horseback to protect his back from the enemy's arrows.

The boy who is to shoulder the horo is called 'Horo-shoikko,' or a horo bearer. Four horo-shoikkos, two from each of the two parties of the parishioners' society, participate in the celebration. Wearing make-up, and beautifully dressed up, the four boys get together at Hachiman Jinja Shrine carrying, on their backs, heavy horo decorated with paper flowers. A horo weighs seven to nine kilograms. After visiting the shrine, they start marching in the shrine grounds.

At the very moment, some young men appear wearing big shishi-gashira (獅子頭), or the head of a sacred imaginary lion-like beast, and start to run with great vigor. They run back and forth three times between the Torii (鳥居) entrance gate of the shrine and the tabisho (旅所), or the temporary shrine specially set outside the precincts for the festival.

It is believed that if little children have their heads bitten by the shishi-gashira head, they will grow up healthy. So people carrying their babies rush toward the shishi, the boy wearing shishi-gashira head.

After this, festival reaches the climax with the tinkle of bells, then the four horo-shoikko boys start to walk in a specially stylized way of walking called roppo (六方　a special way of walking of Kabuki [歌舞伎] play).

As it always rains on the festival day, they chant:「雨がフルヤの八幡さま」, meaning "The rain in Furuya stays mainly on the Hachiman Jinja shrine."

* The word「フルヤ/foo-roo-yah」is a pun, having a double meaning of "furuya": "the name of the neighborhood (Furuya　古谷)" and "to rain (furuya　降るや)."

Kinome Choja
木野目長者

Once upon a time, in the village of Kinome (木 野 目), there lived a very wealthy man named Sugiyama (杉山). All the people in the village respected him very much, and called him Kinome Choja (木野目長者 The Philanthropic Billionaire of Kinome), not Mr. Sugiyama. He lived in a huge mansion comfortably well supplied with many people to work for him. And he had such large fields. Though he was such a wealthy man, he was so beneficent and kept good company with everyone unbiasedly. So he was liked by a lot of people.

In a certain year, since there was a continuous downpour and the districts on the Ara-kawa river (荒川) were affected by flooding, all peasants suffered from extensive damage. They ran out of what little food they had saved and some were dying from hunger.

On hearing the news, Kinome Choja readily gave all the food he had stored to the starving people — rice, wheat, vegetables, and so on. And furthermore, he, by giving them jobs, encouraged those suffering peasants who were discouraged and depressed by the series of uneasy famine. The work he provided was the civil engineering project to build more and stronger levees and mounds along the river, in order to protect their lowland areas from floods.

The villagers, blessing him for his favor, honored him and called him Kinome Choja-sama (木野目長者さま Our dearest Kinome Choja, Billionaire).

The mansion called Kinome Choja's has already disappeared. It is said that Minami Furuya Elementary School stands on the site of Kinome Choja's estate.

Also, Mr. Kinome Choja is said to have believed in Kan'non (観音 Bodhisattva of Mercy) and to have housed an image of Kan'non in a small temple called Rokkakudo (六角堂 the Hexagonal Temple).

Shishi-no-Miya Shrine and Mochi Rice Cake
獅子の宮さまとお餅

Located on the Shingashi-gawa river (新河岸川), the village of Furuichiba (古市場 = Old Market) in Minami-furuya area (南古谷) was once a bustling marketplace handling a great deal of farm products to be shipped to Capital of Edo (江戸) and abundance of goods were brought from the capital.

One day, since there had been a downpour in the upper reaches, the river rose and many kinds of things were carried down to the village. Then the villagers found something strange coming up and going down in the swollen river. What was that? Oh, it was such a sacred 'shishi-gashira (獅子頭),' or a wooden mask representing the head of an imaginary lion-like animal called ' 獅子 =shishi.'

The people in the village picked it up in a hurry. And then they built a shrine and enshrined the shishi-gashira as 'The God of Shishi-no-Miya Jinja shrine."

From that day on, every night, there came a young stranger to the village and played around. He was, in fact, the shishi-gashira that had transformed itself into a young man. But the villagers, never recognizing him to be a shishi (獅子 an imaginary creature like a lion), enjoyed playing with him every night.

Now it was around the end of the year. People started pounding steamed rice into mochi (餅) rice cakes for the New Year at every house in the village. The young man, attracted by their work wanted to join them and helped them. After pounding mochi, he tried a piece of soft and sticky mochi for the first time in his life. Unfortunately, however, it was stuck in his throat because he did not know how to eat it. He suddenly began to tumble about in agony. After having a great struggle with the mochi in his throat, the poor young man strangely vanished into the blue.

The villagers worried about him so much that they made every effort to look for him. Finally, they found out that the young man was an incarnation of the shishi-gashira that was enshrined in the Shishi-no-Miya shrine.

Afterwards, the people of Furuichiba village made it a rule never to eat mochi rice cakes on the first five days of the New Year, they say.

Jihei-Zuka
次兵衛塚

Once upon a time, in the village of Suna-shinden (砂 新 田), there lived a man whose name was Jihei (次兵衛). Since Jihei and his wife had no children, they visited many temples and shrines and prayed to gods to give them a child. Unfortunately, however, they were not blessed with any children. And then, they thought it was the last chance to pray for gods' help, and decided to go and visit the God of Lake Haruna-ko (榛名湖) in Gunma Prefecture (群馬県), which was famous to be responsive to prayers for rain. For days, they stayed there and prayed earnestly. Their genuine wish was realized at last, and a lovable baby girl was given to them by the God. Instead, they made a promise to return the child to the God of Lake Haruna-ko when she became seven years old, because she was a child of the God.

Jihei-san (次兵衛 さ ん Mr. Jihei) was so glad and so delighted having a daughter that he was unconscious of the passage of time, completely forgetting that their daughter had already become seven years old. At that time, as he noticed something unusual in her manner, Jihei observed his daughter carefully. He then found that the 'zori (草履)' straw sandals were drenched every morning. That reminded Jihei of the promise he made with the God of the Lake Haruna-ko, and he immediately took his daughter to Lake Haruna-ko. On arriving there, Jihei's daughter dived into the lake, turning into a big snake. A woman, her attendant, changed into a crab and cleaned up the lake. That was why there were no fallen leaves in and around Lake Haruna-ko, they say.

Jihei-san, feeling very sorry for his daughter, dug a hole in the ground and shut himself up in it, and kept on chanting a Buddhist sutra until he finally died. The spot is called Jihei-Zuka (次兵衛塚 The Tomb Mound of Jihei), and it is believed that if you visit the mound and pray, you will be kept safe from the hail damage.

Inemuri-Zuka
いねむり塚

A portrait of Ono-no-Komachi (小野小町) is among the set of Portraits of the 36 Poets called 'Sanju-roku-Kasen Egaku (三十六歌仙額),' which is dedicated to Toshogu Shrine (東照宮). Ono-no-Komachi, who was a well-known poet and has been a synonym for a beauty, was a woman living in about the middle of the 9th century in the early Heian Period (平安時代 794-1192). She is said to have had some connection with Kawagoe (川越).

Very long ago, Ono-no-Komachi was on her travels to visit various places throughout the country. When she came to the place called Fujima (藤間) near Kawagoe, Ono-no-Komachi saw a cozy-looking forested mound at the roadside. She decided to take a rest there for a while. As soon as she sat down, a surge of tiredness might have caught up with her after a long trip, she unintentionally dozed off while resting against a tree. For a while, she was sound asleep, being unconscious of the passage of time.

The noise that people were making woke her up. When the people saw the woman who woke out of sleep, they were so surprised at her beauty that they lost their voices. They were only gazing at her with rapture. Ono-no-Komachi immediately left that place and went away to continue her travel. The people of the village, learning the woman was Ono-no-Komachi, spoke of her beauty again. And in order to immortalize the mound of the incident, they decided to name it 'Inemuri-Zuka (いねむり塚)' which means 'The Mound Where Ono-no-Komachi Dozed.'

People said that visiting the mound would cure people of serious diseases. They also said that women would be beautiful if they washed their faces with the water from the nearby spring which they called 'Kesho-no-I (化粧の井 /keh-show-no-ee/),' meaning 'The Spring of Cosmetic.'

Oiteke-Bori
おいてけ堀

The area, in Naguwashi Village (名細), where the Koaze-gawa River runs, had been swamps full of ponds and deeps since both the Oppe-gawa River (越辺川) and the Iruma-gawa River (入間川) flow nearby. So the fish living there were numerous and anglers visited there continuously.

One day many years ago, a peasant went there in order to fish hearing of the reputation. He found deeps that looked like a good fishing point. He cast a line and began fishing. Soon he overjoyed that he perpetually caught fish one after another as rumor said. When dusk was falling, his creel was filled with fish, so he stopped fishing and walked up the bank to go home.

Then he heard an eerie voice howling from the spot where he had been fishing. "おいてけ！ (/ oh-ee-tay-kay / Leave them behind.) おいてけ！ (Leave the fish behind in the deep (堀)." The peasant thought it was his mishearing and started to walk. "おいてけ！ (Leave the fish behind in the deep.)" This time, the voice was clear enough for the peasant to hear.

"Damn it！ Who in the world orders me to leave the fish I caught?" he thought.

He unwillingly took one fish out of his creel, threw it into the water and started to walk home again. Then the voice howled even eerier than before.

"おいてけ！ おいてけ！ (Don't take them!)"

The peasant did not want to, but he was so fearful that he had to leave behind all the fish in the creel and ran away from the place without looking back.

After that, the peasant would never go fishing in the deeps again. Never again, they say.

Exchanging Eggplants at Osuwa-sama Shrine
おすわさまのなすとりかえ

The Suwa-jinja Shrine (諏訪神社) in Fujima village (藤間) is called 'Osuwa-sama (おすわさま)' and is loved very much by the local people. On August 27th, in high summer, at Osuwa-sama shrine, the ritual of 'exchanging eggplants' is held annually.

A long time ago, there lived a vigorous young man in the village. But strangely, when summer came every year, the lad became sick. He had to stay in bed very often and was troubled because he could not work. The young man was at a loss as to what to do. His family were also worried about him and tried every possible means to make him better, but in vain. So they finally visited Osuwa-sama shrine in the neighborhood and prayed to the God.

Then that night, the God of Osuwa-sama appeared in his dream to announce to him, "Eat an eggplant grown in the field, and you will get well."

Soon he followed the divine message in the dream and ate an eggplant. Then, the lad suddenly got well enough to work like mad. After that, every time summer arrived, he ate eggplants.

This miracle became known to everybody in the village. People began to offer to Osuwa-sama three eggplants harvested in the year and to receive one from Osuwa-sama in return.

The performance of this act is said to have become the practice to prevent people from getting sick in the summer season.

This annual event of 'exchanging eggplants' is held on August 27th at every Suwa-jinja shrine in the neighboring areas. It is, however, held on August 28th at Osuwa-sama in Tsuruse City (鶴瀬市). This is because Osuwa-sama of Tsuruse, being hard of hearing, misheard the date of the event which was fixed at the conference of Osuwa-sama Gods from the neighboring areas, they say.

Bunzo'emon, A Friend of Crying Children
泣く子もだまるぶんぞうえもん

There once lived in Masukata Village (増形), a very rich man named Bunzo'emon (ぶんぞうえもん). He served as the chief village head of the community of the eight neighboring villages. When the Tokugawa shogun (徳川将軍) came hunting in the area from Edo (江戸 Capital, present Tokyo), he always used Bunzo'emon's mansion as his lodging.

On that occasion, the shogun saw Bunzo'emon's daughter by chance and fell in love with her. So the shogun recommended Bunzo'emon to make her his maid in the castle in Edo. Feeling it was a distinct honor to be asked so, Bunzo'emon soon made his daughter attend the shogun. And his family prospered more and more after that.

One day, Bunzo'emon visited his daughter at Edo-jo (江戸城) Castle, and on his way back home, he passed by Kamekubo Village (亀久保). Since he traveled in a fine kago (駕籠 a covered palanquin) accompanied by several followers, the procession was quite a decent one. As soon as they caught sight of the procession, the villagers went on their knees on the ground and bowed. And the parents stealthily pinched their children's buttocks. Then the children burst out crying with pain.

On hearing them crying, Bunzo'emon made the procession stop and scattered many coins of temposen (天保銭 an oval shaped copper coin with a square hole in the middle) on the ground.

"Oh, poor little children, don't cry. Stop crying for these coins," said Bunzo'emon gently and scattered coins again.

The story of this event spread throughout the area, and

85

everybody began to do the same.

Even children began to chant:

> "Handsome and generous Bunzo'emon
> Makes a crying child smile, smile, smile!"

It is said that the shogun at Edo-jo Castle, hearing of the rumor, complained, "Oh, no! Bunzo'emon pours out money like water. It's no use giving him money. That's the limit!"

From that time on, Bunzo'emon's family rapidly fell into decline, they say.

Hakusan-sama of Masukata
増形の白山さま

Hakusan-sama (白 山 さ ま), the Gurdian Deity of Hakusan Shrine (白山神社) in Masukata Village (増形) has been believed to be a goddess since old times. This shrine's festival is held three times a year: in April, July and October. (The July festival is specially called Ten'no-sama 天王さま).
At every festival, they perform okagura (お神楽 sacred music and dance performed for gods). They say that the shrine's grounds are crowded with people at each festival.

Once upon a time, they held an amateur sumo (相撲 sumo wrestling) tournament as a festival entertainment in its grounds. However, strange to say, all the men who participated in the sumo tournament suddenly began to suffer from a stomachache and stayed in bed.

At the following festival, the villagers, forgetting completely what had happened in the previous festival, decided to perform shishi-mai dance (獅 子 舞 dance wearing a shishi-gashira mask). Some people prepared everything necessary for the dance, and they started dancing to the merry music of bamboo flute and drums. But this time again, all the men who joined in shishi-mai dance suddenly had a stomachache and had to stay in bed. Since such strange things happened in a row, the villagers began to say that Hakusan-sama was a goddess, and so she hated something rough and wild. And they decided never to perform sumo bouts or shishi-mai dance in front of Hakusan-sama. The villagers believe that if they break the agreement, they will surely suffer from a stomachache or a plague.

In April, in the neighboring village of Hirakata (平方), shishi-mai dance is held. But it is said that the villagers of Masukata never permitted even the shishi-mai dancers from Hirakata Village to pass through their village.

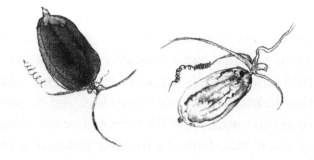

The Sixty-Six Burial Mounds in Matoba
的場六十六塚

There were lots of kofun (古墳 ancient burial mound) in Matoba Village (的場), Kasumigaseki (霞ヶ関), as the local people used to say, 'The Sixty-Six Burial Mounds in Matoba.' Among them, the largest one is 'Ushi-zuka Mound (牛塚).' This is the biggest 'zenpo-koen-fun (前方後円墳 tumulus in the shape of an old-fashioned keyhole: meaning literally 'a square in the front and a circle at the back') in Kawagoe. Many relics, the articles buried together with a dead body, were excavated from the tumulus. This Ushi-zuka Mound is said to have been built in the early seventh century. According to the legend of Ushi-zuka Mound, the place around the tomb mound used to be green grazing grounds where cows were pastured. And it was here that they buried the dead cows. The huge keyhole-shaped tumulus, seen from a distance, looked just like a lying cow, and so the people in the neighborhood came to call it Ushi-zuka Mound (The Cow Mound).

Another is O-Ise-zuka Mound (お伊勢塚). In the Edo Period (江戸時代 1603-1868), people wanted to go a long way and visit 'Ise Jingu Shrine (伊勢神宮)' in Mie Prefecture (三重県), but only a few people were allowed to go there because of the strict restrictions. So, they built a branch shrine of Ise Jingu Shrine on this knoll and visited it instead. People then called this mound O-Ise-zuka (お伊勢塚), meaning 'The Mound of Ise Jingu Shrine.'

Miyoshino-zuka Mound (三芳野塚) is said to have been the original place where the Miyoshino Jinja Shrine (三芳野神社) had once been built, which was situated in the grounds of Kawagoe-jo Castle (川越城) during the Edo Period. Hatsukari-zuka (初雁塚),

Hata-zuka（旗塚）, Ko-zuka（旧塚）, Mato-zuka（的塚）, Nuka-zuka（糠塚）, Bah-zuka（ばー塚）, Kanabori-zuka（金堀塚）, and tens of nameless kofun tombs are said to have been in its neighborhood. That is why the place where these kofun tombs existed was called 'The Sixty-Six Burial Mounds in Matoba.'

The area stretching from Matoba to the villages of Uwado（上戸）and Nakaosaka（中小坂）is well-known for many kofun burial mounds, many of which are thought to have been built from the sixth to the seventh centuries. The artifacts excavated from these mounds are extremely fine and valuable.

Kompira-sama-no Tengu
こんぴらさまの天狗

There is a small shrine called 'Kompira Dai-gongen (こんぴら 大権現) at Joshiki (上式) in Kasahata Village (笠幡), and it is said to be one of the branch shrines of 'Kompira-gu Shrine (こんぴら宮) in the Shikoku district (四国).

Once upon a time, when the villagers were fast asleep in the dead hours of the night, a sudden strange noise was heard, "Bari-bari-dot-sheen!"

"What is it? It cannot be the thunder at this time of the year," a villager said to himself. Then again, there was a louder noise than the first one, "Bari-Bari-Dot-Sheen!"

"Wah-hah-hah-hah-hah!" somebody was laughing loudly.

The next morning, the villagers gathered round and buzzed with excitement about the strange noises, "I heard strange noises." "So did I." "Yeah, me too."

So they went to the hill at the back which the big sound came from. There they found many big boughs of Japanese cedar trees were broken.

"Who on earth did this?" one man said.

"I'm sure last night's laughter came from the direction of the Kompira-sama Shrine," another said and others agreed, "Yep"

They went to the shrine together. What a shame! They felt very sorry to find the doors of the worship hall of the shrine left open, and that the main shrine was in a terrible mess.

"I guess Mr. Tengu (天 狗 an imaginary red-faced, long-nosed monster of human with supernatural power), the messenger of the Kompira God did it. He must have been very angry with us for leaving the shrine in disorder and untidy like this, without coming here to clean it."

So they immediately started to clean the inside of the shrine buildings and its grounds. The villagers are said to have promised each other, "We'll surely clean the shrine once a month from now on."
No one in the village heard the noises of trees falling down or the laughter ever after, they say.

This shrine's festival is held on October 9th and 10th every year.

Yonaki Jizo — san
夜泣き地蔵さん

From the crossroads of the Koma-kaido highway (高麗街道), in Kasahata (笠幡) area, there runs Sen'nichi-do road (千日道). Somewhere on the road near to Kamijuku (上宿), there stands a stone statue of Jizo Buddha (地蔵) called Yonaki Jizo-san (夜泣き 地蔵さん).

Long ago, there was a very happy family in Kurohama (黒浜) Village. The mother had a baby at the breast, so she took the baby wherever she went. And furthermore, since the baby was an only child, the parents loved their child very much. Speaking of worries with their baby, there was the only one that annoyed them. That was 'yonaki (夜泣き crying at night).' Without any special reason, the baby cried badly in the middle of the night. The parents were worried about it, and took their child to the doctor to see if anything was wrong with it. But the doctor could not find any problems. They tried every possible means to stop the baby crying in the night. But none of them worked well. And the crying at night was getting worse and worse than ever.

Then one day, as the mother had some work to do in Kamijuku Village, she was walking toward it bearing the baby on her back. On the way, she happened to see many people gathering at the roadside. She wondered what was happening there. So, she went up to one of them and asked her why people were gathering there.

"Ah, this Jizo-san has the power to cure the diseases of children. And we are all here to pray to him," the woman replied.

On hearing the good news, the mother knelt down right in front of the stone statue of Jizo-san, and prayed with all her might. She kept visiting the Jizo statue to pray for — three times seven — yes, for twenty-one days. When the twenty-one-day prayer was completed, wonderful to say, the baby suddenly stopped crying in the night, and grew to be a stronger and healthier child than before.

This story made 'Jizo' statue famous, and people began to call it 'Yonaki Jizo-san,' meaning 'Jizo-san, the Guardian of the Children Crying at Night.'

People say that they offered mud dumplings when they made wishes, and offered white rice dumplings when their wishes were fulfilled.

A Tale of the Koaze-gawa River
小畔川のはなし

The river running right through Kasahata Village (笠 幡) is called the Koaze-gawa River (小畔川). This river is said to have been quite a troubled one. Whenever there was some rain, the river soon overflowed the banks and fields, washing away bridges and running winding in different directions. So the villagers called it 'The River Koaze-gawa with 99 Bends (小畔九十九曲がり).'

Here is an old tale. The villagers once talked about building a sturdy bridge across the river.
"What kind of bridge shall we build?"
"How about building it up with stone?"
"Yeah, it must be strong and durable."

So they decided. And they bought a lot of big pieces of hard stone and built such a fine stone bridge that no one had ever seen before.
"Now we don't have to worry about the bridge any more even when it rains heavily."
They were so delighted and celebrated the completion hand in hand.

But one night they heard stones break with a crash. All the villagers, startled, went with torches in their hands toward the place around which the sound came from. What did they find there? That massive stone-built bridge was completely broken into pieces. They examined the bridge's rubble carefully and found the track of a gigantic snake. The villagers wondered what had happened but could not understand. Even after that, they again and again built bridges of stone, every one of which was broken.

"Oh, I've got it! The Giant Snake of the Koaze-gawa River hates stones, I'm sure."

From then onwards, they decided to build bridges not of stone, but of wood.

That was why there had been no stone bridges over the Koaze-gawa River.

Hitotsume-Kozo of the River Koaze-gawa
小畔川の一ツ目小僧

Long long ago, there lived a wise Buddhist priest in the small village of Kujirai (鯨井). His name was Zenku (善空) and he was loved and respected by the villagers because of his wisdom and virtue.

One day, after he had done his business somewhere outside the temple, he was hurrying back to his temple along the lonely road. When he came to the River Koaze-gawa (小畔川), it had already been pitch-dark and he had to light his way with chochin (ちょうちん , 提灯 paper lantern). Then he heard an eerie voice calling his name, "Zeng-ku-u-u! Zeng-ku-u-u!" from behind.

"Well, who is it calling me at this late hour?" he wondered and looked back, but there was nobody there.

"Ah, it must have been my mishearing because of the wind," he thought to himself and started walking in the dark. Then again he heard the same voice calling him, "Zeng-ku-u-u! Zeng-ku-u-u!" But this time the voice called his name very clearly.

"Who on earth is calling me?" He turned around and was astounded to find a towering, monstrous hitotsume-kozo (一ツ目小僧 a one-eyed monster) standing in front of him. The monster grinned with its mouth wide open as if it were ready to swallow him in one gulp. Shuddered with horror, Priest Zenku ran away at full speed back to the temple.

Later that night, Priest Zenku reflected himself and was very much ashamed of being terrified at the apparition of hitotsume-kozo, neglecting his duty as a Buddhist priest. He soon got back to where he had seen the monster. He called, in a loud voice, to hitotsume-kozo that was often frightening the villagers and passersby. Priest Zenku loudly chanted at the monster a holy sutra with all his might and successfully led it to the Suitengu Shrine (水天宮) at Osaka (小坂) on the River Koaze-gawa. He finally enshrined the hitotsume-kozo monster in it.

Kojiro of the Koaze-gawa River
小畔川の小次郎

This is a story of olden days. There lived, in the Koaze-gawa River (小畔川), a giant snake named Kojiro (小次郎) that was very mischievous and naughty.

One day, when he was swimming down the river as usual looking for something to play on, Kojiro saw a handsome boy cutting the grass on the river bank. Kojiro was immediately and thoroughly fascinated by this good-looking boy. The more he looked at him, the more attractive the boy appeared to be. Falling in love with the boy, who looked good-natured, at first sight, Kojiro turned himself into a beautiful young girl at once, and went up to him and spoke to him. Although Kojiro tried every means to attract his attention, the boy did not even give a glance at the girl. He indifferently kept on cutting the grass.

Feeling deeply humiliated, Kojiro, disguising himself as a young girl, got furious at the boy. Kojiro angrily took away the kama (鎌 a sickle) the boy was using, and disappeared into the river with it.

That is why the nearby bridge came to be called Kamatori-bashi Bridge (鎌取橋), meaning 'the bridge where a sickle was taken away.'

After that, in the Koaze-gawa river, a terrible roaring sound was heard right before floods. And when the river was swollen, a big pale fireball sprang up from its surface and drifted along over the river.

"Out comes angry Kojiro there!
Out never go, young guys, never!"

Said the villagers as soon as they saw the pale fireball.

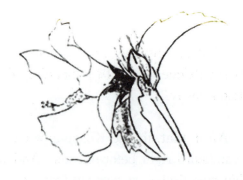

A Story about the Toge-Bashi Bridge
とげ橋のいわれ

Once upon a time, there lived a giant god called 'でえだらぼう (Deidarabo /day-dah-rah-bow/),' who was good at creating mountains. While he was walking all over Japan, he sometimes took a rest sitting on the top of Mt Fuji-san (富士山), and made two mountains of Mt. Nantai-san (男体 Mt. Male) and Mt. Nyotai-san (女体 Mt. Female) of Mt. Tsukuba-san (筑波山).

At a certain time, he was supposed to make a mountain in the Chichibu area (秩父). On the way there, he happened to pass by the village of Naguwashi (名細) in Kawagoe (川越). He stumped along, "Clump! Clump!" leaving large hollows in the ground behind him as his footprints.

When he just came near to the Koaze-gawa river (小畔川), he suddenly cried out, "O-o-ouch! and squatted down in pain on the ground. What a thing! A little splinter had got stuck in the sole of his foot. Even 'Deidarabo' was not able to take another step forward because of the pain. He immediately pulled out the splinter from his sole, and thrust it into the middle of the river. Then he headed for the Chichibu area.

In those days, the Koaze-gawa river was winding and even wider than today, and sometimes it became very wild. Wanting to cross the river easily and safely, the villagers had been thinking of building a bridge over the Koaze-gawa river. On that occasion, some villagers were surprised to find a big stake was stuck in the middle of the river. Soon they gathered the whole village to the spot, and they built a fine bridge making use of the stake.

Later, they realized that that stake was in fact the splinter which got stuck in Deidarabo"s sole. People were most grateful to Deidarabo for his splinter, and named the bridge Toge-bashi (刺橋 The Splinter Bridge).

This stake of the splinter was never washed away even when floods raged.

The Hackberry Tree with Warts
いぼ榎

There was once a Buddhist temple dedicated to Fudo Myo'o (不動明王), the Deity of Fire, in Shimo-osaka Village (下小坂). It was called ' 北向き不動 (/key-tah-moo-key-foo-doe/ The Image of Fudo Myo'o Facing North). At the back of the Fudo Temple, there used to be a tall and big hackberry tree, people say. The surface of the trunk was so rough with many dents and knots which looked like warts. In those dents, there always stayed some rainwater. People said that the hackberry tree was fairly old.

Here is an old legend about this hackberry tree which goes:

If you suffer from warts, the first thing you've got to do is to visit and pray to Fudo Myo'o. And then wash your hands with the rainwater in the dents on the hackberry tree. Touch the warts with ' 割り箸 (wari-bashi /wah-ree-bah-she/ disposable half-split wooden chopsticks) and chant "Warts, warts, Cross the bridge!" three times. If you practice that for a few days, then the warts will suddenly disappear. Very strange.

This wart-curing power of the hackberry tree was so popular that wari-bashi chopsticks were always placed around the tree.

* Japanese words meaning 'bridge (橋 hashi, -bashi)' and 'chopsticks (箸 hashi, -bashi)' are homonyms. They sound similar. "Warts, warts, cross the hashi (/hah-she/ a pun: meaning a bridge and chopsticks).

It is said that this hackberry tree was used, in the old days, as a milestone measuring one 'ri (里 about 4 kilometers),' and was located just one 'ri' away from Fuda-no-Tsuji crossroads (札の辻 the crossroads where official notice boards once stood), the center of old Kawagoe Town.

In addition, at a certain time, the villagers used the hackberry tree as a fire tower to overlook the whole village, hanging a fire bell from it.

Now the hackberry tree is gone.

Kappa's Visit to the Ise Jingu Shrine
かっぱの伊勢まいり

A long time ago, the three naughty kappa (か っ ぱ、 河 童 legendary amphibian creature) went on a long journey to visit the Ise Jingu Shrine. They were Kojiro (小 次 郎) from the Koazegawa river (小畔川) in Naguwashi Village (名細), Kesabo (袈裟坊) from Igusa (伊草) of Kawajima village (川島) and Kajibo (かじ坊) from Konuma (小沼) of Sakado Town (坂戸). They were very good friends.

Disguising themselves as well-off tourists, the three kappa had a booze at every post town, eating the most expensive dishes, buying the high-class goods for souvenir at every wayside tea house. They spent money like water, so the shopkeepers began to doubt them.

The shopkeepers made contact with each other, advising, "Be careful of the trio of tourists who are too extravagant."

And they checked the coins the trio used very carefully and finally found out the coins were in fact 'the lids of tanishi (田にし /tah-nee-she/ a mud snail or a snaillike shellfish living in muddy water).

Once a cheat came out, a tumult came about. The three tourists were chased by shopkeepers and caught at last. After their true character of kappa water imps was revealed, all the three kappa were scolded terribly and tortured.

After that, the three kappa imps became quiet and obedient, and never went on a journey again, they say.

A Shugenja monk and a Fox
しゅげん者と狐

Here is an old story. Behind the Hie Jinja Shrine (日枝神社) in Uwado Village (上戸), there used to be a forest where trees grew so thick that it was very dark even during the day. People say that there lived many mischievous foxes that fooled people.

One day, a shugenja (しゅげん者、修験者 a monk who trains himself by walking or running around in fields and mountains) was walking through the forest, when he saw a fox nodding in a doze at the root of a tree in the light of day. He thought he would tease it just for fun.

"Hey! Watch out! Here comes a hunter!" he shouted and threw a pebble at it. The fox was frightened out of its wits and ran away for its life.

"Ha, ha, ha!" the shugenja monk proudly laughed at it. "Who's afraid of the big bad fox? How stupid of you to be tricked by man, you silly fox!"

When night fell, a stranger covering his head and cheeks with a tenugui (手ぬぐい) hand towel suddenly came to the shugenja's house. He said, "Dear sir, a friend of yours is suffering from a sudden illness near Matoba Village (的場). Please be quick and come with me."

The shugenja left home at once following the stranger. Very fast walked the stranger, who veiled his face with a tenugui, and the shugenja sometimes had to beg him to slow down, "Say, wait, please!" But the man kept on walking so fast that the monk could hardly keep up with him. The shugenja, being anxious about losing his way to his sick friend, walked and walked desperately,

106

but could not catch up with the stranger. The shugenja almost lost the sight of him, when the eastern sky was growing light at last. Even the shugenja himself, who was good at walking and running in the mountains, felt very tired and said, "Oh, boy. I'll have a little rest now." He sat down and looked around very carefully. Then, to his great surprise, he found himself in the midst of the forest behind the Hie Jinja Shrine which he had walked through in the daytime.

That fox, which was fooled by the shugenja in the daytime, got mad at him, and took terrible revenge on him, people believed.

The Set of Bowls of the Bottomless Pond
底なし沼の膳椀

Kitaya-no-numa (北谷の沼), the pond in a small village of Shimo'osaka (下小坂) is also called 'the Bottomless Pond.' At the corner of the pond, there is a hole of one meter in diameter. It is called 'Okama (お釜 a kettle)' and is believed to be the opening for a giant snake of Tachiagari-no-Matsu (立上がりの松 the Rising Pine Tree) growing in the grounds of the Igeyama Inari Shrine (会下山稲荷).

From olden times, the Guardian Spirit of the Pond had been well known to be generous enough to lend as many bowls and cups as the villagers wanted on the occasions of celebrations.

One day, a villager was in trouble because he had no sets of bowls to use for the guests at a celebration to be held at his house. Hearing about the Bottomless Pond from the elders of the village, he thought how lucky he was and hurried to the pond.
"May I ask you a favor, my dear Spirit of the Pond? Please lend me the sets of bowls and cups for twenty people," he requested.

Early the next morning, he went to the pond. There! There were exactly twenty sets of bowls and cups placed on the margin of the pond. He happily brought them home and successfully finished the feast.

When he was going to return those bowls and cups to the pond, he found one bowl missing. He counted them again and again, only to find one bowl was missing. Feeling troublesome, he did not apologize to the Spirit of the Pond for losing a bowl. He shamelessly put the rest of the bowls and cups on the edge of the pond without compensating the missing one.

The Spirit of The Pond was infuriated at the villager's rudeness, and from then on the Spirit would turn down even the villagers' earnest requests. It would never lend any sets of bowls and cups to anybody again, they say.

Ibo Jizo-san
いぼ地蔵さん

Once upon a time, a very honest and hardworking peasant lived in Terayama Village (寺山). Though the Iruma-gawa river (入間川) sometimes rose and burst the bank and overflowed the houses and fields, he lived a life of ease every day with nothing special to worry about.

However, if there was one thing he could not stand at that time, it was 'ibo (いぼ wart).' At first he had one alone on the back of his hand. But it spread to his feet without notice, and then to his face at last. He could not stand it any more, and went to the doctor. Unfortunately, even a doctor could not cure his warts at all. Then he could think of nothing but praying to gods to help him, and visited shrines and temples here and there. But his warts never cured.

One day, when he was walking along the Matsuyama- kaido (松山街道) highway and came to the village of Minami- yamada (南山田), he saw a stone image of Jizo-Bosatsu Buddha (地蔵菩薩) standing at a crossing as a guidepost. He thought this was the last chance to get well, and he prayed to it seriously. "Please cure me of warts, Mr. Jizo."

Then, the next day, to his surprise, the warts he had suffered from were all gone. Again and again he felt his body to see if there were any warts, but he found none.

"The Jizo I prayed to yesterday must have helped me," he thought. So he instantly went to the Jizo to say thanks, taking some hot green peppers from his field.

This story became popular among the neighbors, and they called the Jizo 'Ibo Jizo-san (いぼ地蔵さん Mr. Jizo who cures Warts).

People from places near and far came to the Jizo one after another to pray to him. It is said that hot green peppers were always offered to 'Ibo Jizo-san.'

Goze-bashi Bridge
ゴゼ橋

The small bridge built between Mizukubo (水久保) in Aina-shinden (安比奈新田) village and Kashiwabara (柏原) in Sayama City (狭山市) is called Goze-bashi (ゴゼ橋).

In the past, at some time around April 14 and 15, the farmers absented themselves from work and spent those two days merrily joining the festivals of the nearby shrines.

And from the villages of Yoshida (吉田) and Kujirai (鯨井), goze (ゴゼ、瞽女 a blind female entertainer who earns money by singing songs playing the shamisen – 三味線 – a three-stringed banjo-like instrument) came to the villages, usually in a group of 4 or 5 people. They sang songs and told stories to entertain the villagers.

Then one day, as they were walking along the road which paralleled the Iruma-gawa river (入間川) and were crossing the narrow wooden bridge at Mizukubo, Aina (安比奈) village, a goze, a blind female entertainer, dropped into the river by accident and drowned.

The spot is said to have been the moat of Shiroyama Fortress (城山砦) in Sayama City and it was a sheer and deep glen. All the goze, blind entertainers and the villagers felt sorry for her, and in cooperation with each other, built a solid bridge with stone at the spot.

Then, the bridge came to be called the Goze-bashi (ゴゼ橋) bridge, people say.

Kita-muki Fudo-sama
北向き不動さま

It happened a long time ago. At the roadside of the highway called Chichibu-kaido (秩父街道) running through Shimo-osaka (下 小 坂) village, there stood a stone statue representing Fudo Myo'o (不動明王 the Deity of Fire).

One day, a horse with a full load of packs was walking by, when it was about to pass the very front of the Fudo-sama statue, it suddenly stopped and would not move at all. The packhorse driver wondered what happened to the horse.

"Well, let's see … What's wrong with the horse? Is it hungry?"

He gave it some food right away, but his horse did not start walking. In fact, it crouched down on the spot and was trembling. The driver tried different ways to make it walk doing this, that and others. He soothed it, threatened it and scolded it. But the horse would not step forward. The driver could think of nothing but making it step back to take another road. And then, the horse began to walk lightly as usual as if there had been nothing wrong.

After that, all the horses and even cows stopped when they came to the front of the Fudo-sama stone statue on the Chichibu-kaido highway. The villagers thought it very strange, and consulted the elder in the village on the matter. He then said it was because the Fudo-sama statue was throwing a fierce look toward the road. So they soon turned the face of the statue to the opposite direction.

That was why people began to call the statue "Kita-muki Fudo-sama (北向き不動さま)", meaning "Dear Fudo Myo'o Facing to

113

the North."

Ever afterwards, horses and cows would walk in a calm manner without stopping at the statue, they said.

Mr. Tengu of the Kosaiji Temple
広済寺の天狗様

Long long ago, most houses in the town of Kawagoe were not built in kurazukuri style (蔵造り clay-covered fireproof architecture), so even a small fire rapidly spread and became a big blaze. People had a lot of trouble dealing with fires in those days.

In Kita-machi neighborhood (喜多町), on the northern rim of the town, there is a time-honored temple called Kosai-ji (広済寺). Its compound used to be like a dense forest with many old trees growing there. One old cedar tree, amongst them, was very tall and it stood out conspicuously. A tengu (天狗 an imaginary red-faced, long-nosed monster of human having supernatural power) is said to have lived in this tree, watching over the town carefully all the time.

One day, there was a fire, and it began to spread fiercely in the twinkling of an eye. It would surely become a big fire. Suddenly the tengu appeared on the old cedar tree from nowhere, and stood on the top of it holding a big fan of feathers in his hand. He strongly fanned and fanned and fanned to turn the wind. He finally swept the fire out of the town, so saving the town from being burned down.

People say that whenever a fire broke out in the Town of Kawagoe, 'Mr. Tengu of the Kosai-ji Temple (広済寺の天狗様)' always came out and guarded the town from fires.

Shabuki-Babah
しゃぶきばばあ

In Kitamachi (喜多町) neighborhood in Kawagoe, there is a Buddhist temple with a history named Kosaiji (広済寺). In the grounds of this temple stands a unique stone image. People call it Shabuki-Babah (しゃぶきばばあ).

Long ago there lived a ronin (浪人), a masterless samurai, in Kitamachi neighborhood. One night, when he came back home, he was very surprised to find a strange stone statue in the middle of his room. He wondered who left such a thing there and why. Not knowing the answer, he took the figure to the Kosaiji temple the next morning, and set it in its precincts.

A little while later, a young daughter of a nearby cotton dealer's came to the Kosaiji temple and happened upon the stone figure. She had been suffering from a bad cold for a long time, and on that day again she was visiting temples and shrines wishing away her cold. For some reason, the young girl prayed to this stone figure, too, saying, "Please help me recover from a bad cold soon." She prayed and made a vow to visit the statue for a prayer every morning for one hundred days to come. And as a sign of her vow, she wound a straw rope around the stone figure.

Miraculously enough, on the hundredth day, her bad cold was completely cured. Wahoo! She was absolutely delighted with the recovery, and offered some tea and kompeito (コンペイ糖、金平糖 confetti) to return thanks to the stone statue.

That came to be the talk of the town, and many people suffering from whooping cough and cold visited the stone image and bound it with straw ropes until at last it became invisible under the ropes. In addition, the offerings of tea and confetti were piled up in front of it.

Shabuki-Babah (しゃぶきばばあ Coughing Auntie) stone image stands in the compound of the Kosaiji temple even today, along with a stone image of the Chinless Jizo Bosatsu (あごなし地蔵さま), which is supposed to be responsive to prayers of worshippers having a toothache.

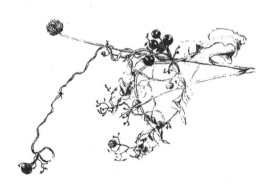

EXTRA: Two different version of a story: 民部稲荷
Minbu Inari Fox Shrine (民部稲荷) -A-

This is an old story. At a certain Buddhist temple in Hachioji (八王子 in Tokyo) lived a young training boy bonze named Shinbochi (新発地). Every night he would go out somewhere, which made the head bonze worried about him. And so the head asked the young trainee where he went.

"To tell the truth, master, I would visit Mr. Minbu at his mansion to the west, and I was treated to dinner and had a chat with him," the boy answered.

The head priest thought that there were only mountains in the west of the temple, and that there couldn't be any houses at all. He wondered at what the young priest's said, but told him, "If the person is so kind to you, I really want to appreciate his kindness. Why don't you invite him to the temple?"

On the following night, Mr, Minbu came to the temple accompanied by his attendants. The head bonze served dinner, and expressed his gratitude for Mr. Minbu's kindness.

As they drank sake, they both began to boast to each other. And they finally agreed to make Mr. Minbu's attendants and the temple servants wrestle. But the attendants of Mr. Minbu were so strong that the temple servants could not win even a single bout.

The next morning, while the boy bonze was sweeping the garden, he found lots of pieces of red and white hair were scattered. He was surprised at them, and could hardly wait for the night. When the night came, he hurriedly went to see Mr. Minbu. Then Mr. Minbu said, "I'm not a human being but a fox

living in the mountains. I really enjoyed the gathering forgetting myself last night. But my fellow foxes knew that I became friends with human beings, so that I can't live here any longer. I'm going to run away toward Kawagoe (川越)."
Saying so, he disappeared.

That Mr. Minbu is the Minbu Inari Fox Shrine in Shintomi-cho (新富町) neighborhood, and is also called Sumo (相撲) Inari Shrine. It is believed to be responsive to prayers for healing bruises. People offer the ema (絵馬) votive picture tablets with the picture of sumo wrestlers on when they pray to the god.

EXTRA: Two different version of a story: 民部稲荷
Minbu Inari Fox Shrine (民部稲荷) -B-

Once upon a time, at a certain Buddhist temple in Hachioji (八王子 in Tokyo), Tama County (多摩郡), lived a young training boy bonze. The young boy would go out every night to enjoy chatting with Mr. Minbu (民部様) at his mansion which was about 800 meters away to the west of the temple, he said.

The head bonze thought it strange that there was no such mansion, but only the range of mountains in that direction as far as people could see. So the head told the young trainee to invite Mr. Minbu to his temple once.

Before long, Mr. Minbu came to the temple riding in a palanquin accompanied by twelve or thirteen attendants. After chatting about various topics, Mr. Minbu earnestly boasted of his attendants' skill as sumo wrestlers, which incited the head priest to make his bonzes wrestle with the attendants of Mr. Minbu. Now bouts started, then Mr. Minbu's followers, who were all small, thoroughly beat the bonzes.

And the next morning, a lot of pieces of red and white hair were scattered on the ground where sumo wrestling bouts were played on the previous night.

In this way, Minbu Fox, whose identity was revealed, knew he wouldn't be able to associate with human beings any more. He decided to move to Mt. Bonshin-yama (梵心山) in Kawagoe (川越), Iruma County (入間郡), about 40 kilometers to the northeast. Mr Minbu, the fox, said goodbye in tears to the boy priest who came to see him. And the fox offered the boy a heaping pile of koban (小判) oval gold coins on the tray as a token of his thanks.

This is the folktale of Minbu Inari Fox Shrine (民部稲荷神社) which used to be in Bonsin-machi (梵心町 一 present 2 chome of Shintomi-cho 新富町 2 丁目) neighborhood. It is said that if you have faith in this Inari Shrine, you will surely be rich, and also this shrine is believed to be responsive to prayers who suffer from bruise and sprain. So it is custom at this shrine to offer the ema (絵馬) votive tablets with pictures of sumo wrestlers on as a sign of thanks when your wish is realized.

『川越の伝説』 『続 川越の伝説』

発　行　川越市教育委員会
編　集　川越市教育委員会社会教育課
挿絵・文　池原昭治

本書は『川越の伝説』『続 川越の伝説』から
61 篇を選び、翻訳しました。

Kawagoe Legends　川越の伝説

2024 年 11 月 10 日　第 1 版第 1 刷発行

発　行　川越を英語で歩こう会
監　修　宮内茂
　　　　〒 350-0034
　　　　埼玉県川越市仙波町 2-15-1　ヘボン塾内
　　　　TEL・FAX　049-222-1710

発　売　仙波書房
　　　　〒 350-1304
　　　　埼玉県狭山市狭山台 2-17-28
　　　　TEL　04-2968-8195
　　　　FAX　04-2909-9395
　　　　URL　https://www.semba-shobo.com/

印　刷　株式会社イシダ印刷

ISBN　978-4-910500-51-5　C0039